Elizabeth George Speare

Twayne's United States Authors Series
Children's Literature

Ruth K. MacDonald, Editor

TUSAS 541

Elizabeth George Speare. *Photograph courtesy of Houghton Mifflin Company.*

Elizabeth George Speare

Marilyn Fain Apseloff
Kent State University

Twayne Publishers • New York
Maxwell Macmillan Canada • Toronto
Maxwell Macmillan International • New York   Oxford   Singapore   Sydney

Elizabeth George Speare
Marilyn Fain Apseloff

Copyright © 1991 by Twayne Publishers.

Twayne Publishers
Macmillan Publishing Company
866 Third Avenue
New York, New York 10022

Maxwell Macmillan Canada Inc.
1200 Eglinton Avenue East
Suite 200
Don Mills, Ontario M3C 3N1

10 9 8 7 6 5 4 3 2 1

The paper used in this publication meets the minimum requirements of American National Standard for Information Sciences— Permanence of Paper for Printed Library Materials, ANSI Z39.48-1984. ♾™

Printed and bound in the United States of America.

Library of Congress Cataloging-in-Publication Data

Apseloff, Marilyn
    Elizabeth George Speare / Marilyn Fain Apseloff
        p.   cm. — (Twayne's United States authors series : TUSAS 541)
    Includes bibliographical references and index.
    ISBN 0-8057-7636-2
    1. Speare, Elizabeth George — Criticism and interpretation.
    2. Children's stories, American — History and criticism.   I. Title.
    II. Series.
    PS3569.P396Z65   1991
    813'.54 — dc20   91-36762

*To Roy, Stan, Glen, and Lynn Susan,
who were always eager for a story*

Contents

Preface

Elizabeth George Speare has written two books that have won Newbery Medals—the award is given to "the author of the most distinguished contribution to literature for children published in the United States during the preceding year"—and one Newbery Honor Book, which also won the first Scott O'Dell Award for Historical Fiction; she also received the 1989 Laura Ingalls Wilder Award for "a substantial and lasting contribution to children's literature," an impressive achievement for any writer but especially for someone who has written only four novels for children. Surprisingly little has been written about her. There are reviews, comments in children's literature textbooks and in some articles not specifically about her, speeches connected with her awards in various editions of *Horn Book Magazine* and in *Newbery and Caldecott Medal Books: 1956–65,* and information about her life and writing in *More Junior Authors, Something about the Author, Children's Literature Review,* and *Twentieth Century Children's Writers.* Nevertheless, for a two-time Newbery Medal–winner, more criticism should exist. In addition to the novels, Speare has also written two nonfiction works about the colonial period and a novel for adults. Earlier writings include articles and one-act plays. All of her work will be considered here.

In many reference works Speare is either discussed slightly or omitted entirely. For example, in the recent *Oxford Companion to Children's Literature* by Humphrey Carpenter and Mari Pritchard, she is given short shrift, a mere seven lines that mention only her two award winners, which are not cross-listed. In contrast, Esther Forbes, another writer of historical fiction with an even smaller output for children (one novel and one biography), has her Newbery Medal winner, *Johnny Tremain,* cross-listed. It is given lengthy treatment, and pertinent information about the author is included. Interestingly, Margery Fisher, in her book *Who's Who in Children's Books,* includes an entry on Daniel from *The Bronze Bow* but makes no mention of Kit from *The Witch of Blackbird Pond,* a more popular book. The same curious selection occurs in Eden Ross Lipson's *The New York Times Parent's Guide to the Best Books for Children.*

The exclusions are surprising. Speare is entirely omitted from the *Dictionary of Literary Biography*'s new volume, *American Writers for Children since 1960: Fiction,* even though her second Newbery Medal–winner, *The Bronze Bow,* was published in 1961 and her Newbery Honor Book and Scott O'Dell Award winner, *The Sign of the Beaver,* appeared in 1983. She is not discussed in *Touchstones: Reflections on the Best in Children's Literature,* although Esther Forbes is included, nor is she discussed in *Writers for Children: Critical Studies of the Major Authors since the Seventeenth Century.* These omissions are a disservice to a writer with the talent of Elizabeth George Speare; her skills are made apparent in this volume.

Certainly no writer is without flaws during the course of a career, especially one of long duration. Although Speare's career began late (she was almost 50 when *Calico Captive,* her first novel, was published in 1957), it has spanned almost three decades so far (*The Sign of the Beaver,* her last book, was published in 1983). Despite some literary faults and a relatively small output, she has won sufficient critical acclaim to warrant more attention and respect. My aim is to show that Speare has frequently and undeservedly been overlooked and that, at times, such as with Jason Epstein's acerbic comments in "Good Bunnies Always Obey" (he calls the Nancy Drew and Tom Swift books superior) and Vivian J. Scheinmann's unflattering essay on Speare in *Twentieth Century Children's Writers,* she has been the recipient of harsher condemnation than is justified.

In this volume, I take a close look at all of Speare's work, including selections from her early plays and articles, the adult novel *The Prospering,* the nonfiction *Life in Colonial America,* and the booklet *Child Life in New England, 1790–1840,* which she produced for Old Sturbridge Village in Sturbridge, Massachusetts. In the context of these works I discuss the strong moral values evident in her novels and the distinctive elements of her style. Furthermore, I also argue that her receipt of the Scott O'Dell Award and her creation of good historical fiction with strong themes has helped to arouse more of an interest in historical fiction for children. This genre, which has seen a decline in readership for more than a decade, deserves a better fate, for it can bring history to life for readers far more than their textbooks can.

Not only has Speare led her readers into other times, bringing those periods vividly to life through memorable characterization and fully realized settings, but she has also given her readers large issues to think about within her attention-holding plots. Because the values presented in the novels are lasting ones, a child may see similarities between the past and the present: he or she may realize that courage, for example, knows no time boundaries. She has presented colonial America objectively, showing the merits of Indian culture skillfully, especially in *The Sign of the Beaver* and *The Prospering.* Also in *Beaver,* two of the characters read *Robinson Crusoe* together; Speare's novel may therefore lead the reader to that classic survival tale as well as to other books about the colonial period.

In addition to reading the primary sources and investigating the usual biographical studies, critical essays, and reviews about Elizabeth George Speare, I interviewed her at her home in Easton, Connecticut, in July 1989, enjoying lunch there afterwards. Later she answered questions through letters as well as during a long telephone conversation. In addition I had long conversations with her first editor at Houghton Mifflin, Mary Cosgrave, who worked with Speare on *Calico Captive* and *The Witch of Blackbird Pond* and who told me a great deal about Speare's early work. I spoke at lesser length with Speare's second editor, Walter Lorraine, who sent me the original cover for *Witch.* Matilda Welter, the senior editor of children's trade books at Houghton Mifflin, sent me a videotaped interview set in Wethersfield, Connecticut, the setting of *Witch,* and provided two photographs and a great deal of other help. Karen Mix of the special collections department at the Mugar Memorial Library at Boston University sent me copies of letters from publishers to Speare and a list of Speare holdings donated to the library.

Spurred on by Speare's extensive research for her novels, I looked into some of her sources on my own. Some of these included *Penobscot Man* by Frank Speck, a book Speare used for both *Beaver* and *Captive*. I studied the Connecticut charter and events surrounding it that Speare refers to in *Witch,* and I obtained a copy of Susanna Willard Johnson Hastings's narrative of her capture (along with her family and others) by Indians and the subsequent trials that they endured for four years. Examining the narrative gave me an opportunity to see how Speare was able to move from the real to the imagined, interweaving both skillfully. My reading of Edward Everett Hale's *A New England Boyhood* showed me how perceptive Speare was in her selections from that volume. Indeed, looking at even just a few of the numerous documents Speare perused made me appreciate her use of the material. She told me how difficult it had been sometimes to relinquish information she especially liked but which would not have added to the narrative; I came to know firsthand what she meant. Yet she is not merely a writer of escapist literature, bringing only the past to her readers; in exploring universal problems and offering timeless values, she offers them hope for the present and the future as well.

There frequently are some unsung heroes who have helped to make books possible, and I have my share of them to thank. The cooperation of Elizabeth George Speare made my job much easier, and my conversations with her first editor, Mary Cosgrave, added greatly to my knowledge of Speare's work and personality. Most important of all was my uncomplaining husband, Stanford, who gave me his excellent advice, help, and careful reading of the manuscript.

Because of an unusual number of computer breakdowns and problems, I owe special thanks to Ray Craig at Kent State University for the many hours he put in trying to find out what was wrong and retrieving as much as possible of my material. He was also my WordPerfect mentor, always able to come up with quick answers to my numerous questions. Allan Plastow provided other essential computer help.

Mike Cole in the interlibrary loan department at Kent State University located and retrieved the books that gave me a glimpse of the kind of research Elizabeth George Speare undertook and an understanding of the type of selections she made from those and many other sources.

Karen Mix of the special collections department in the Mugar Memorial Library at Boston University provided me with copies of the materials Elizabeth George Speare had donated to her alma mater, giving me a chance to compare some manuscripts with the finished novels and to see what changes editors may have suggested that were or were not carried out.

I owe a special debt to my loving father; although he did not live to see the completion of any of my books, he always knew that I would write one. He offered me his support and encouragement for many years and looked forward to hearing about each work's progress. He would have been pleased and proud to see this third book in print.

Acknowledgments

Excerpts from *Calico Captive* by Elizabeth George Speare. Copyright © 1957 by Elizabeth George Speare. Reprinted by permission of Houghton Mifflin Company.

Excerpts from *The Witch of Blackbird Pond* by Elizabeth George Speare. Copyright © 1958 by Elizabeth George Speare. Reprinted by permission of Houghton Mifflin Company.

Excerpts from *The Bronze Bow* by Elizabeth George Speare. Copyright © 1961 by Elizabeth George Speare. Reprinted by permission of Houghton Mifflin Company.

Excerpts from *The Sign of the Beaver* by Elizabeth George Speare. Copyright © 1983 by Elizabeth George Speare. Reprinted by permission of Houghton Mifflin Company. Reprinted also by permission for British Commonwealth rights of Victor Gollancz Ltd.

Excerpt from *The Prospering* by Elizabeth George Speare. Copyright © 1967 by Elizabeth George Speare. Reprinted by permission of Houghton Mifflin Company.

Excerpts from *Child Life in New England, 1790–1840* by Elizabeth George Speare. Copyright © 1961 by Elizabeth George Speare. Reprinted by permission of Old Sturbridge Village.

Excerpts from *Life in Colonial America* by Elizabeth George Speare. Copyright © 1963 by Elizabeth George Speare. Reprinted with permission of Random House.

Letters from Mary Silva Cosgrave to Elizabeth George Speare. Reprinted with permission from Mary Cosgrave.

Letters from Anne Barrett to Elizabeth George Speare. Reprinted with permission from Houghton Mifflin Company.

Letter from Walter Lorraine to Elizabeth George Speare. Reprinted with permission from Walter Lorraine.

Letters from Mary Silva Cosgrave and Anne Barrett to Elizabeth George Speare from Elizabeth George Speare Collection, Boston University Libraries.

Chronology

1908 Elizabeth George born 21 November in Melrose, Massachusetts, the first of two children of Harry Allan and Demetria (Simmons) George.

1926–1927 Attends Smith College; father dies.

1927 Transfers from Smith College to Boston University.

1930 Receives B.A. from Boston University.

1930–1932 Teaches English at the Chamberlain School in Boston, Massachusetts.

1932 Receives M.A. from Boston University.

1932–1935 Teaches high school English in Rockland, Massachusetts.

1935–1936 Teaches high school English in Auburn, Massachusetts.

1936 Marries Alden Speare on 26 September; moves to Wethersfield, Connecticut.

1939 Gives birth to son, Alden, Jr., 25 December.

1942 Gives birth to daughter, Mary Elizabeth, 27 April.

1949 Publishes her first magazine article, "Don't Be an Armchair Eskimo," in *Better Homes and Gardens,* in December.

1953 Writes *The Anchor: A Play in One Act for Four Women,* produced by amateur dramatics group, Wethersfield, Connecticut.

1955 Writes *The Stranger: A One Act Play of Bible Times,* not performed.

1953–1956 Works part-time at the University of Connecticut interviewing disabled homemakers and writing pamphlets on handicapped homemakers for the home economics program.

1957 Writes *Calico Captive*; writes "Abby, Julia, and the Cows" for the June issue of *American Heritage.*

1958 Writes *The Witch of Blackbird Pond*. *Calico Captive* is named an American Library Association Notable Children's Book of 1957.

1959 *The Witch of Blackbird Pond* is awarded the Newbery Medal and the Society of Colonial Wars Award.

1960 *The Witch of Blackbird Pond* is added to the International Board on Books for Young People (IBBY) Honour List.

1961 Writes *Child Life in New England, 1790–1840*; moves to Easton, Connecticut.

1961 Writes *The Bronze Bow,* which is named an ALA Notable Children's Book.

1962 *The Bronze Bow* is awarded the Newbery Medal.

1963 Writes *Life in Colonial America.*

1967 Writes *The Prospering,* a novel for adults.

1983 Writes *The Sign of the Beaver.*

1984 *The Sign of the Beaver* is awarded the Scott O'Dell Award for Historical Fiction and the Child Study Association Award; it is also named a Newbery Honor Book.

1989 Receives the Laura Ingalls Wilder Award for "a substantial and lasting contribution to children's literature."

1

Life, Imagination, and Art

Most writers, especially those who concentrate primarily on books for children, begin producing their creative works when they are relatively young—in their twenties or thirties—but there are always exceptions. One of the most noted was Laura Ingalls Wilder, born in 1867, whose first book, *Little House in the Big Woods,* did not appear until 1932, marking the beginning of an illustrious career. Although Elizabeth George Speare did not, as Wilder did, create historical fiction from her own life, there are parallels to be drawn between these two authors. Speare began writing at an early age, yet her major accomplishments were achieved beginning in her late forties (a youngster compared to Wilder) and continued into her seventies. Speare drew her material not from her own past experiences but from diligent research and a lively imagination. She was to follow in Wilder's footsteps by writing her novels (and some nonfiction) when her children were in junior high school and thus less dependent on her. Mary Silva Cosgrave, Speare's first editor, observed that "Mrs. Speare and Mrs. Wilder share many of the same qualities—both have high moral principles, integrity, a gift for storytelling, and a natural style of writing."[1] It is most fitting, then, that eventually Elizabeth George Speare earned the Laura Ingalls Wilder Award for "a substantial and lasting contribution to children's literature."

Childhood and Education

Elizabeth George's Massachusetts childhood was "an exception-
ally happy one,"[2] filled with family reunions and a love of the New
England outdoors "where we hiked and picnicked."[3] In woodsy
sections of Melrose, the city where she was born in 1908, the family frequently would hike on Sundays.[4] Since Melrose was only
about 10 miles north of Boston, family treats included visits to
the big city to attend plays and concerts. Summers were spent at
Marshfield Hills near Scituate, a town about 30 miles south of
Boston on the way to Cape Cod, "where we stayed on a hill with
a breathtaking view of the ocean. . . . I had endless golden days
to read and think and dream, and it was then that I discovered
the absorbing occupation of writing stories" (*MJA*, 189).

As a child she was constantly writing, encouraged by her parents. "I can't recall any specific criticism. I am sure my mother
must have had many suggestions, but I remember only the encouragement and a ridiculous pride in my unremarkable efforts."[5]
Speare further recollects that "my parents enjoyed reading aloud,
and one of my earliest memories is of going to sleep with the
sound of their voices reading Dickens."[6] Speare's favorite book as
a child was Frances Hodgson Burnett's *The Secret Garden*. When
she began to experiment with her own writing, her first efforts
were realistic stories and imitations of legends (Letter 1); she
shared her creations with a cousin whenever they got together.
Her writing continued through high school where her extracurricular activities were concentrated in dramatics. "I was probably
somewhere in every play we produced in high school, not ever a
lead. I did play the role of Yum Yum in a quite pretentious production of *The Mikado*" (Letter 2). Although she never wrote any
plays for high school, she "did write a pageant for the Camp-Fire
Girls" (Letter 2), a New York publisher. Later she "had some one-
act plays published by Baker's" (Letter 1). One of them, "The
Anchor," was put on in Wethersfield with an all-woman cast. She
did not pursue dramatics in college, but she was on the editorial
staff of the literary magazine at Boston University (Telephone
conversation).

Speare attended Smith College in Northampton, Massachusetts, until her father's sudden death in September 1926, after
which she transferred to Boston University to start her sopho-
more year. She and her mother took an apartment on Commonwealth Avenue near the university, and in 1930 she received her
B.A. in English. "After I graduated from Boston University I divided my time between teaching in a small private school in Boston [Chamberlain School, where she taught from 1930 to 1932]
and studying in graduate school, running the three blocks between classes" (Booklet). After she graduated from Boston University in 1932 with an M.A. in English, she taught high school
English (Shakespeare and Browning) for four years in Rockland
and Auburn, Massachusetts towns near Boston. Speare found
teaching in public schools "far more challenging and rewarding
[than at the private school], but not always enjoyable" (Letter 1).
Her stint at Rockland was during the Great Depression, and
Rockland was a factory town. The high school boys wanted to be
out earning money in the factories, but there were no jobs to be
had. As a result they were in school, which did not interest them,
and they were often unruly. Speare had a hard time coping with
their behavior because she was not a good disciplinarian. Fortu-
nately for her, her next position at Auburn was in a newly opened
school with enthusiastic children, "just paradise" after her Rockland experiences (Telephone conversation). Her background in
English was to serve her well in the future, for her later written
work was to need very little editing for language errors or style.

Marriage, Family, and Early Writing

Elizabeth George met Alden Speare through her brother. "Alden
and I met when he and my brother, both in college, were working
for the summer at a Boston University athletic field. When I
wanted to borrow my brother's car I drove them both to work, and
presently we were planning picnics and other foursomes" (Letter
2). After her marriage to Alden on 26 September 1936 in Newton,
Massachusetts, Alden's birthplace, the couple moved to Wethers-

field, Connecticut, which would become the setting for *The Witch of Blackbird Pond*. Speare got a job with the YWCA in neighboring Hartford right after her marriage. She could not continue to teach or even to substitute because even as late as 1936 the law there forbade the hiring of married female teachers (Telephone conversation). Soon she became a mother, first to Alden, Jr., a Christmas baby born in 1939, and then to Mary, born 27 April 1942. Once their schooling began she became very involved in their school, in their extracurricular activities, and in family outings like those of her childhood, such as picnics and trips to the city. "Any family can fill in the record of the next fifteen years, crowded with piano practice and dancing school and camping and orthodontists and PTA and Cub Scouts and Brownies" (Booklet). Family skiing and fishing trips were also numerous. The latter, not always stimulating for Speare, led her to libraries in the fishing locales, where she began to do more serious writing than she had been doing up until then.

Helen Reeder Cross said in her biographical note at the Newbery and Caldecott Medal Awards Banquet for *The Witch of Blackbird Pond* that Speare's "winters were spent doing her stint as Cub Scout den mother and as a teacher in the Sunday school, and included endless miles of chauffeuring, children's partying, and the careful typing of her twelve-year-old son's neighborhood newspaper for which he was reporter, editor, printer, and publisher."[8] Cross also stated that home, rather than writing, came first for Speare, ". . . [her] husband and two teen-aged children . . . fill her heart and most of her time" (Cross, 78). This love of family surfaces in all of Speare's subsequent novels and makes it less surprising, in retrospect, that she was doing no serious writing during this busy and important growing-up period in the lives of her children.

Helen Cross and Speare were members of "the Quill Drivers," a group of women who all wanted to write. It was formed by Speare, Helen, and another friend, and it consisted of about eight members, "all scattered now" (Letter 1). "The Quill Drivers probably began to meet in the early fifties. . . . We continued to meet until both Helen and I moved from Wethersfield [1961]. I think

we were more of a support group than a serious critical group—
all of us beginners and grateful for enthusiasm and encouragement. . . . In such a group members go riding off in all directions,
each one wanting to write her own story. Chiefly, the group kept
us working, and every one of us succeeded in publishing in one
field or another" (Letter 2). As Helen recalled, "Elizabeth Speare
claims to have been inspired by the give-and-take of the group"
(Cross, 78). Certainly she felt the need of their opinions and reactions, even if she did not follow any suggestions that may have
been made, for while she was writing both *Calico Captive* and *The
Witch of Blackbird Pond* she read pieces of each to the circle (Letter 1).

With more time on her hands once her children were in high
school and remembering the adage that you should concentrate
on what you know best, Speare began to write magazine articles.
"Most of the articles were short stories which appeared in small
religious magazines such as the *Christian Home*. Some were written under another name. They paid one or two cents a word, but
it was a thrill to see one's name in print. One or two articles [ap-
peared] in [the *New England*] *Galaxy*, the Sturbridge magazine"
(Letter 2). The article writing continued. "Mainly they were about
the things that filled our own lives at this point—doing things
with children, vacations, making Christmas presents (I once won
a trip to Bermuda on this one), and answering children's questions about life" (Letter 2). One of her friends from the Quill Drivers suggested that she try writing for magazines: "It was Helen
Reeder Cross who first introduced me to these possibilities—she
was very successful at them" (Letter 2). Cross said that these
were Speare's "'Helpful Hannah' articles, based on child-rearing
techniques" (Cross, 79). She had many rejections, but she perse-
vered, and her articles were published little by little. "The first
one to be published ["Don't Be an Armchair Eskimo"] appeared in
Better Homes and Gardens. It was an article on the family skiing
together long before skiing was at all popular—how to start children on skis" (Letter 1). Another of her articles, "Outwitting the
Therbligs," accepted by *Woman's Day* magazine, advised homemakers on how to manage their time and energies better, "a

rather pioneering idea about 1953" (Letter 1). "This was the article that led to my work at the University of Connecticut" (Letter 2). This part-time work went on for a few years and consisted of "doing publicity and articles on handicapped homemakers" (Letter 1). Although she was eventually offered a full-time position with the university, the timing was wrong. She had submitted the first three chapters of *Calico Captive* to Houghton Mifflin. "I never worked full time at the University of Connecticut. I had finally agreed to take a regular position when Mary Cosgrave of H[oughton] M[ifflin] asked to see the rest of *Calico Captive* and I resigned at once" (Letter 2). Speare also wrote "an article, 'Suppose Your Child Runs Away,' for *Parents*" (Letter 2) and "an article for *American Heritage* about our sister town of Glastonbury" (Cross, 81) that appeared in June 1957. Even after the publication of *Calico Captive,* other articles appeared in print, "many in obscure and religious magazines" (Letter 1). Speare called these "fillers." In addition to these writing activities, Speare "also had the one-act plays published by Baker's" (Letter 1) and another published in *Plays.* All of the early writing was a preamble to the novels that would eventually completely overshadow the other pieces.

The Productive Years, 1955–1983

Speare usually wrote while her children were in school, using first the dining-room table and then their rooms as her temporary study.[9] Because she was New England born and bred, it was not surprising that eventually she began to explore some of the region's historical documents and narratives in libraries when she became bored on fishing trips. Not until she happened upon the story of Susanna Johnson, a chapter in a book on the Connecticut River by Walter Hard, did the creative spark fully ignite. She located the 1807 edition of the diary at Trinity College, where she spent hours copying sections (the book could not be taken from the library) from the tale of Susanna Johnson's ordeal after she and her family were captured by Indians (Telephone conversation). That was also the beginning of Speare's fascination with American history.

It was not Susanna, the author of the captivity narrative, but her younger sister, Miriam Willard, a shadowy figure in the diary, who captured Speare's imagination. "Finally I began to write down her adventures, filling in the outlines of the actual events with new characters and scenes of my own creation" (Interview). Realizing that she needed to know much more about the period, Speare began her research. "Gathering material for a book takes me a year or more. While I am taking notes in libraries and museums, the story is slowly growing in my mind. . . . I work very slowly, doing only a few pages a day, trying to make each sentence say what I mean" (Interview). She spent about three hours a day on her writing (Interview). Despite such care with her daily work, Speare routinely made three drafts of each of her novels: "When I finish, I go back to the beginning and type it all over again, changing as I go. . . . The third time I type it to send to the publisher, and I don't let anybody else type it because I keep changing it all the way through, and I want to catch little things as I go. . . . I don't mean that I rewrite every page" (Interview). Unfortunately, in the process of rewriting, Speare "destroyed each page [of the previous draft] as I typed" (Letter 2). After the publisher suggested changes, those were made, and that version became the final draft of the manuscript; there was no more rewriting. Before it went to the publisher, her daughter, Mary, listened to the chapters each evening and offered her comments and criticisms. "When *Calico Captive* was finally published in 1957, it was dedicated to her" (Booklet). The following year, *Calico Captive* was chosen as an ALA Notable Children's Book of 1957.

Speare's second book, again historical fiction, was set in Wethersfield, the Connecticut town where she had lived for 20 years. Although she spent months reading her state's history for a second spark for her imagination, none came. In her comments in *Children's Literature Review,* Speare recounts what happened next: "Then gradually I became aware that some people were waiting, not in the pages of history but in my own mind. . . . Each of these people began to take on sharper outlines, individual dimensions . . . long before I had found a place for them to live or a time in which they could be born. Finally I was compelled to find a home for them."[10] It should be noted that when Elizabeth was in school and college, history was not her favorite subject. She was not alone in that attitude. Jean Fritz, writer of biographies and historical fiction for children, has stated in her essay "The Very Truth" that, "as every survey shows, history is not a popular subject with children" even though history "is the very *stuff* of life."[11] As a teenager, Speare was no exception in her disinterest in the subject.

The result of Speare's imagination and more research was *The Witch of Blackbird Pond* (1958), such a well-written novel that her editor, Mary Cosgrave, found almost nothing to object to, nothing of substance to change. It was Speare's first novel to win the Newbery Medal, and it showed an obvious improvement over *Captive* in the handling of characters, plot, and theme. Fritz has said that "scholarship may be the first requisite that . . . a writer of history should display, but . . . an ability to translate the past into spirited, human terms is equally important" (Fritz, 85). In *The Witch of Blackbird Pond* Speare was fully able to make such a translation. When asked if she had also read that book in progress to her daughter, Mary, in the evenings, Speare responded negatively; Mary was too busy then (Telephone conversation).

Two more books followed quickly, both very different from *Witch*. *Child Life in New England, 1790–1840* (1961) and *The Bronze Bow* (1961) were dissimilar from the first two novels, for *Child Life* was a nonfiction booklet, one of a series put out for the restored Old Sturbridge Village, while *The Bronze Bow* was set in Palestine at the time of Jesus.[12] With the latter, Speare wanted to create a special novel, but not one set in colonial America. Even the impetus for *The Bronze Bow* was unlike the impetus for the others; this time Speare wanted to write a story for Sunday-school children that would humanize Jesus (Interview). Having her own strong faith, she wanted to impart some of her feelings for Jesus to children so that he would seem more reachable and more human and would therefore have more of an impact on their lives. The book won a second Newbery Medal for Speare, and it was widely read in public schools, not just in Sunday schools as she had envisioned.

Speare's next effort was a nonfiction book that Chanticleer Press asked her to write. This project presented a new kind of challenge for her, because she had to meet a deadline for each chapter, not at all her usual way of working. The result was *Life in Colonial America* (1963), which was well received. Four years later her one book for adults, *The Prospering* (1967), appeared to good reviews. Then she was silent for 16 years until *The Sign of the Beaver* (1983) was published. Like *Calico Captive,* it grew out of a real incident Speare read about; this time the story took 20 years to germinate and come to fruition. The novel was again noteworthy, another award winner.

During the period before and after the publication of *The Sign of the Beaver,* Speare was busy traveling to see her children. "Our son was in Taiwan four years ago [1985] and he was in Jakarta for two years. We got to see him in both places. . . . We traveled every year for a long time" (Interview). Later, in a letter, Speare expanded on her travels: "En route to Taiwan, we stopped in Hong Kong, Japan, and Hawaii. We went to Kenya and Tanzania on an Audubon safari. While in Jakarta, where our son was work-ing for the government helping to set up a population survey . . . we joined a small group visiting Sumatra which had just been opened to visitors, and spent a night in a remote village where we were welcomed with a royal procession of all the villagers, feasted in the long house and entertained by a historical drama acted by torchlight" (Letter 2).

Speare's other vacation journeys were to Greece, Rome, Israel, Norway, Sweden, Denmark, Costa Rica, England, Scotland, and Wales (Letter 2). On one of those yearly trips Speare finally was able to visit the Holy Land. In Egypt she took "a wonderful boat trip down the Nile" (Letter 2). She never did visit Montreal, one of the principal settings in *Calico Captive.* There were the regular skiing and fishing trips, too, including travels to Switzerland "several times in the winter where I walked about the villages in the snow while my husband skied" (Letter 2) and visits with grandchildren. Although her writing of children's novels temporarily ceased during this period, Speare worked for five years on a biography of Fanny Kemble for adults that was never published. After that, "I don't think I did any other writing before the Beaver" (Letter 2). Despite her assertion that "I am ashamed to admit how lazy I was" (Letter 2), Speare was outwardly very busy until the anecdote about the boy in the Maine woods waiting for his family to return began to grow more firmly in her imagination and began to demand research and writing.

Past and Present

Speare has been asked why she chose to write historical fiction. Her reply offers young readers solid reasons why they should include such books in their reading in addition to the fantasy, adventure, and realistic fiction tales that young readers are particularly fond of: "I have discovered now that when I follow the adventures of an imaginary family through some great events of the past the pages of the history books come alive for me. I always find in my study of earlier days a new understanding of the present, and I come back to the things which I know best with fresh perspective. I think that one of the great gifts which the past has given to all of us, young and old, is this reenforcement of the spirit" (Booklet). The present generation did not spring up out of nothing. Its nurturing is influenced by the previous generation, as was their parents'. Whether those living in the present like it or not, the past is always in some degree a part of the present and future. As Milton Meltzer observes, "While history is not everything, it is an aspect of everything. It makes us aware of the character of our own time by helping us to see it in comparison and contrast with another."[13] Meltzer adds that the child "needs to know that the past as well as the present holds meaning. . . . The historian, in recollecting and patterning past actions of people and societies, sometimes makes it possible for the child to find his [or her] bearings in the bewildering currents of human diversity" (Meltzer, 90). The past provides stability and direction for a contemporary child who may be discouraged and dismayed by the numerous possibilities ahead from which a future path must be chosen.

Although Speare continues to travel and has said that she has no other subject in mind at the moment for another novel (Interview), who is to say what historical anecdote that she happens upon as she browses in some library or museum might not inspire her once more to create characters and scenes? Her readers can only hope and wait.

2

Beginnings

Speare's early publications, the articles and plays, are important to look at briefly for style in order to observe what development occurred between those pieces and the novels that would bring her acclaim. Although they would not be expected to have the depth nor the range of descriptive style of her four books for young readers and her adult novel, nevertheless the articles point to a clarity of expression from the beginning and an interesting readability that would appear later in her nonfiction works about colonial life. The plays reveal some of Speare's themes, her attitudes toward religion, and her interest in characters and how they interact.

The Articles

Speare's first published article, "Don't Be an Armchair Eskimo," appeared in *Better Homes and Gardens* in December 1949 under the name of Elizabeth George.[1] In the article she points out the rewards of families, not just children, enjoying winter sports together: "You could not make a better investment in family solidarity, good health, and sheer enjoyment" (*BHG*, 150). She first talks about skating, maintaining that even a two-year-old can participate by using double runners. Then she focuses on skiing, telling the reader that it will provide a child with a lifetime of pleasure and good company. She counters the three main objections to the sport—danger, expense, and inconvenience—with facts. She points out that all sports have dangers if behavior is reckless; children and adults must follow the rules. She acknowledges that there is expense involved, but says that the most expensive equipment is not necessary. Good shoes and bindings are the most important, as well as skis that truly fit. Comfortable clothing that will not restrict movement is also necessary, but such clothing can be used everywhere, not just on the slopes. Often the equipment can be handed down to other family members. Another expense involves lessons, but an instructor is not mandatory; a skiing manual will also serve the purpose. She cites the benefits of learning as a family: "You will be surprised at the pride children will take in your efforts and at the persistence, sportsmanship, and courage which will grow . . . from the happy sharing of failure and skill" (*BHG*, 152). Inconvenience is given short shrift, for Speare says that after the first few times, "it won't matter" (*BHG*, 152). Instead, you will "know a smug pity for all these people who have wasted precious hours indoors. . . . They have not stood on top of a hill, intoxicated by air and sun, and looked out upon a world that is breathlessly beautiful and good. Poor souls, they are not skiers!" (*BHG*, 152). Based on the many skiing outings she had with her own children, the article has a light, humorous tone. Such a tone is evident in her other short publications, even those based upon historical material.

Another article, "Outwitting the Therbligs,"[2] resulted from a course Speare's husband took in motion-and-time study. He appeared in her kitchen one evening after dinner to make notes on the way she did the dishes, and his talk of "therbligs" prompted her to look at his textbook herself to find out what he was talking about. There she discovered that "a therblig turned out to be quite harmless. It is a word coined by Frank Gilbreth . . . to refer to an element of work. It is, in fact, Gilbreth spelled backward—well, almost [not when it is plural]" (*Day*, 35). Speare began to look more closely at her usual routines, discovering that "therbligs could add up faster than calories unless you watched them" (*WD*, 175). She began to have ideas of her own in addition to the tips given in the text, but she also ran into difficulties. One of the tips was to rearrange rooms and equipment so that everything would be in a place "where it is most easily laid hold of when needed. Logically, that is the point nearest to where it will be used" (*WD*, 175). That "prepositioning" became both a game and a challenge, for at times it meant throwing things out that family members did not want to part with.

Scheduling was tackled next, and she was pleased to discover that rest, unavoidable delay, and avoidable delay were all to be included in it. Then "I began to juggle hours experimentally" (*WD*, 176), and gradually her chart took shape. There was still the motion study to contend with, and Speare learned that time spent before tackling a task to get it organized resulted in more of a saving later. She learned new ways to do things such as using two hands to set the table and to dust instead of just one. She gives other specific examples for the homemaker. She also re-counts her failures, the writing tablets placed strategically that always disappeared, her inability to plan a week's menu in ad-vance, and others. However, the end result was positive: "Our days seemed not more regimented, but more leisurely" (*WD*, 176).

The tone of the article is light, with humor surfacing frequently. The result is enjoyable as well as informative. This scheme would be especially useful for working spouses who do not have much time to devote to housework. Since housework is often a chore, and a very repetitive one at that, the quicker a person is able to get through the tasks, the more time there is for relaxation. Al-though this article was published in 1953, its message and sug-gestions are as timely today as they were then.

Not all of the articles were informative in an applied sense where the reader could immediately put suggestions to good use. Speare also wrote articles of a different kind, such as "Abby, Julia, and the Cows,"[3] based on an episode that began in November of 1873 and did not end until three years later. The setting was Glastonbury, Connecticut, a neighboring town to Wethersfield, where two elderly sisters lived. When they found that their property and that of two widows had been reappraised by the all-male council for higher taxes but that no property owned by males had been equally reappraised, they began their protest at the town meeting. From there it escalated to national interest through newspaper accounts of their difficulty (their pet cows were taken to auction to pay the owed taxes), and women's suffrage leaders joined the fray, inviting the two sisters to their convention at Worcester, Massachusetts, where Abby made a speech. Later, when they lost fifteen acres of their pastureland through trickery, they sued the tax collector who was responsible. Although the first verdict was in their favor, the appeal went against them. A second appeal was initiated. "For two years a wide and sympathetic public followed this devious litigation. Across the nation, even in England and France, editors and columnists lauded the Glastonbury cows in prose and poetry. . . . The hospitality, wit, and charm of the two elderly spinsters captivated the world beyond Glastonbury" (*AH,* 57).

The two sisters continued in the spotlight. They "shared honors as speakers at a number of suffrage conventions, got an ovation in Washington, and even appeared at a hearing before the United States Senate" (*AH,* 96). When they went to see the president, they wore "all their clothes at once, simply putting on top, day or night, whatever costume the occasion demanded" (*AH,* 96). Speare chose to include several humorous anecdotes about the three-year episode, revealing her own keen sense of humor regarding the historical happenings. She mentions some of the sources she used (the Springfield, Massachusetts, *Republican,* Lucy Stone's comments in *Woman's Journal,* etc.), working them into the unstilted text so that the reader becomes curious about what else was said or written about the episode that had to be omitted. Speare's ability to arouse curiosity in her readers is a trait that appears in her other, longer nonfiction works and in her historical novels. This article appeared in the same year as but just before the publication of Speare's first novel, *Calico Captive.*

Another article, "Old-Time Schoolmasters and Scholars,"[4] published in the *New England Galaxy,* was a precursor of the booklet she would later do for Old Sturbridge Village, *Child Life in New England, 1790–1840,* which is discussed in a later chapter. The *New England Galaxy* was also published by Old Sturbridge Village; Speare's article dealt with the early 1800s, describing the physical makeup of the schools first with their scanty furnishings and even fewer supplies: "In country schools there were frequently no books for the pupils, only the single primer, the dog-eared grammar, perhaps Noah Webster's spelling book, and the sturdy arithmetic, all of which stayed in the teacher's hands" *(Galaxy,* 7). In the cities more books and subjects were available, including, "surprisingly, the perusal of newspapers" *(Galaxy,* 7). Although one-room schoolhouses were the norm in the country, the stereotype of such schools as having barely enough pupils to fill them is overturned by Speare's description of the first public school to open in Hartford, Connecticut, "considered a model in 1832." It "housed in its four rooms 500 to 600 pupils ranging in age from three to sixteen years" *(Galaxy,* 7).

Several sources are quoted in the article, but it was obviously a custom of the *Galaxy* not to use footnotes. However, a reader who dips into some of the background selections Speare used for *Child Life in New England* will quickly find that Speare examined some of the same books for this earlier article. Alice Morse Earle provided an anecdote about the early precociousness of Timothy Dwight, later president of Yale, that appears in "Schoolmasters" and that is related in chapter 7 of this book. The curriculum at the prestigious Phillips Academy for boys is frequently used as an example of what was studied, as Speare draws not only from Earle's work but from "the memoirs of Josiah Quincy, statesman and in later life president of Harvard" *(Galaxy,* 10). She also uses the diaries of children for sources, quoting sufficiently from them to give the reader a sense of the personality of the writer as well as of the historical circumstances.

Speare informs the reader of the discrepancy between the education of girls and that of their brothers, for even into the nineteenth century girls were not considered worth educating in anything beyond writing and arithmetic, and those subjects were studied only by girls in the best families (*Galaxy*, 11). Although that situation gradually changed, it was many years before girls could take their places in the schoolroom beside their brothers. Speare reveals that schoolmasters were also male in the beginning, a position gradually taken over by females in the nineteenth century because of "a shortage of qualified male teachers" (*Galaxy*, 14).

In this article Speare includes some questions as part of her style, a technique that will reappear in her other, longer nonfiction books. Near the beginning of the article she asks, "What were they really like, those 'dear old golden rule days'? What of the boys and girls who went out from those first schoolrooms to shape the new Republic? And what of the schoolmasters who left their mark upon the future?" (*Galaxy*, 6). She proceeds to answer those questions in the rest of her article. Scattered throughout are illustrations of various kinds: a page from a child's own book; certificates; a picture of Sarah Pierce, founder of the Female Academy in Litchfield, Connecticut; and one of an ideal schoolhouse in an idyllic setting. These illustrative materials came from the museum in Wethersfield that Speare was to draw from for *Child Life in New England*.

The Plays

Speare's first published play was *The Forest of Arden,* written for junior and senior high school students. It is set in London's Globe Theatre in 1602 and is apparently intended to give readers some facts about Shakespeare's theater in an easily digestible form. For example, when one character is unable to perform and his twin sister substitutes for him, the reader learns that male actors then played female as well as male roles. Bonnie, the sister, explains that her father has forbidden both mother and daughter from even attending a performance. Shakespeare is also one of the play's characters, highly pleased with Bonnie's portrayal of Rosalind in *As You Like It*. Speare had been teaching Shakespeare to her students and knew that a short play would make the period come alive for them more readily than reading or hearing a lecture about women in the theater in Shakespeare's day.

The first of Speare's one-act plays for adults, *The Anchor*, was subtitled *A Play in One Act for Four Women*.[5] It begins with "The Story of the Play," a tale of four sisters who meet after 10 years apart thanks to the invitation of Faith, who wants them to come to the old homestead in Vermont. Each thinks "she is the only one invited" (*Anchor*, 4). The story does not divulge what happens; instead it whets the reader's appetite for further reading. The opening scene is in the Vermont farmhouse living room, its description similar to that of rooms in some of Ibsen's realistic plays with the table in the middle of the room, doors leading off to other parts of the house, heavy curtains on the windows, and a fireplace on one wall. The first reference to the title occurs when three of the sisters, recovered from their initial shock at discovering that each was invited, talk about Faith and why their father left her the farmhouse. "Father had those notions at the end. He was determined Faith ought to have the farmhouse—'for an anchor,' he said" (*Anchor*, 8). There are other references to anchor as the play progresses, the anchor shifting from the farmhouse to Malcolm, the British college professor Faith is supposed to be marrying the next day.

The play is a study of the personalities of the four Baxter sisters as they interact. They are distinctive, made to be rather one-dimensional to help keep them straight, and each is described as she enters. Fanny is the first to arrive, "a typical small-town matron" (*Anchor*, 5), naive and always seeming to see the good side of others. Lil, entering shortly after Fanny, is the bitter one, for Faith took her fiancé from her years earlier, and although Lil is now married, her husband is a poor provider and her son is in an iron lung because of polio. Her life is not easy; in fact, she has come with the intention of asking Faith to help them pay some of their hospital bills. Abby, the third to appear, is the eldest, a take-charge person who has her own school, "and none of this progressive nonsense about it" (*Anchor*, 11). Faith, who has arranged this rendezvous, is last because she had to wait for a late train and then a taxi. She, however, seems to be the lucky one despite two failed marriages, for her sisters believe that she is wealthy. They then learn that she has brought them together to attend her third wedding, to a man she feels is her perfect anchor, a college professor from an old English family. Abby has come to be sure that Lil is helped, and Faith, when she learns of Lil's troubles, offers to deed the farmhouse over to Lil, even though their father wanted her to have it. The irony of the situation is disclosed in the second, final scene which takes place the next morning. The living room is transformed into a wedding setting by hard work and forsythia. Faith and Abby have been gone all morning, their errand revealed when Faith gives Lil the deed to the house over her feeble protests. All is well until Faith receives a telegram from Malcolm: she says that he tells her that they must leave tonight after all on the *Queen Mary* where the ship's captain will marry them. All of their work at the farmhouse has been for nothing, for she must now rush to catch a train. After she hurriedly leaves with Lil to get the last train out, Abby discovers the crumpled dropped telegram, and she and Fanny learn the truth: Malcolm has jilted Faith.

Faith, the envy of her sisters, is revealed to be the poorest judge of people of all of them and the one with the most misfortune. A hint of foreshadowing occurs early in the play when Faith reminisces about always being a poor gambler, always making the wrong choices at the county fairs. Abby remembers, "You always had to keep trying. The rest of us learned our lessons and held onto our pennies" (*Anchor*, 12). Because of her own foolishness about men, Faith first lost all of her money by turning it over to her second husband who squandered it and then left her; now she has given up the farmhouse to Lil for all of her troubles. It will enable Lil to free her family from debt, for they can move there and use the money from the sale of their other house to pay the bills. Their future looks bright. Faith is fortunate that she has a job with a travel agency to fall back on. Her father had indeed been farsighted in regard to her, for she was the one most in need of an anchor. These interactions of the Baxter family members are a prelude to the Williams family relationships that will unfold with much more telling effect and depth in Speare's adult novel almost 15 years later, *The Prospering*. Like the novel, the play shows a more serious side to Speare's writing style than appears in her other works. Only Fanny, whose speech is described as being "of the non-stop variety" and "full of little affectations" (*Anchor*, 5), provides a suggestion of lightness. *The Anchor* was put on by a group in Wethersfield while Speare was living there. She wrote of the occasion, "I didn't even know the group was doing it. I only attended . . . one single production."[6]

Another of Speare's one-act plays demonstrates her early interest in both setting and theme that will emerge later in her novel *The Bronze Bow*. In *The Stranger: A One Act Play of Bible Times*, as in the novel, the setting is Palestine at the time of Jesus, and in both a character is filled with hatred and antagonism that Jesus dissipates by his presence. The dialogue reveals that the older son left four years earlier; his departure is the apparent cause of the father's belligerent attitude toward everyone in the village. In *The Bronze Bow*, it is the Roman occupation and what happened to his family that fill Daniel's heart with hatred. In the play, however, Jesus does not appear as he will in the novel. Instead, the reader learns of his influence from the subsequent behavior and comments of the family involved.

The Stranger is a 17-page play set in a "bare room with rough walls"[7] in Palestine and contains six characters. The cast of characters is followed by a one-paragraph synopsis before the one-act play begins.[8] It is divided into two scenes with the same setting. In the first scene the family troubles unfold: the older son, Hamish, ran away four years earlier, and the father refuses to have his name spoken in their home. Jacob, the 12-year-old son, spends all of his time with the camel drivers of caravans, and daughter Ruth, betrothed to David, wants more out of life than the poverty that she sees around her and that she cannot escape in a life with David. Her mother, physically sick with a bad back, is also sick at heart over the departure of Hamish and her inability to talk about him. Matathias, the father, has an evil reputation because of his terrible temper and nasty disposition.

In the first scene, Matathias announces that a stranger will be coming to spend the night with them, and although they have hardly enough food for themselves, Matathias insists that everyone make the stranger feel welcome and not a burden. The scene ends with Matathias telling his family who the stranger is. "His name is Jesus. He comes from Nazareth, and he is a carpenter by trade" (*Stranger,* 10). Scene 2 begins the next morning as the stranger departs, and Matathias decides to accompany him to the crossroads. While mother and daughter are out fetching water, Jacob is visited by Tayma, the merchant with whom the boy bargained for a place in the caravan leaving that day for Jerusalem. When Jacob tells Tayma that he cannot go just then and asks for his gold piece back that he had taken from his father's land savings, Tayma refuses. Then David enters and is surprised to find that Ruth apparently has had a change of heart after Jesus' visit: now she realizes that accumulating wealth is nothing compared to having a loving family, and she is more than willing to marry David. Her mother has also discovered that her back no longer bothers her.

David has news of his own: Hamish has returned. Soon Jacob comes running in shouting the same news. His father's first reaction is, "Your brother Hamish is dead" (*Stranger,* 18). Although his wife tearfully pleads with him, his reply is the same, and he goes outside. Later he learns that Jacob stole the gold piece to leave home but changed his mind, and he is devastated to realize that both of his sons wanted to leave. When Matathias and his family learn that Jesus is talking to a crowd at the crossroads, they decide to go to hear him. Matathias reveals the deep impression that Jesus had on him during the night, and the expectation of seeing and hearing the carpenter once more helps him to make up his mind: he will go and fetch Hamish to hear him, too. His wife weeps for joy as the play ends.

Here is a family torn apart, almost destroyed by anger, just as Daniel's family is in *The Bronze Bow.* Listening to Jesus and talking with him prove to be turning points for both Matathias and Daniel as hatred finally gives way to love. Jesus is not the only one at the crossroads; Matathias and his family are at a turning point also. It is interesting to note that although *The Bronze Bow* is more than 250 pages long, in the novel Daniel's conversion is almost as swift as Matathias's. Because of his sister Leah's precarious hold on life, Daniel has a more pressing need to release his anger, and his acceptance of Jesus' teachings seems less contrived than Matathias's. Matathias says that "something stood in the way" (*Stranger,* 20) of his complete acceptance of Jesus' teachings during the night and morning visit, and that "something" is obviously his anger toward and denial of his son Hamish. When he decides to get Hamish, the door is now wide open for him to accept Jesus fully.

Not only Matathias but all family members are touched in some way by Jesus' visit. Jacob, thought worthless and only fit to work with camels, now believes that he, too, has some skills and has the potential to become a carpenter, after he produces a well-made whistle following Jesus' instructions and is praised by the carpenter-teacher. The mother's release from her back pain and Ruth's change of heart towards her fiancé, David, have already been mentioned. The rapid changes made by the characters in the play are not as successful as the more thoughtful ones made by Daniel's friends in *The Bronze Bow.*

A look at these selections of early works gives the reader a sense of Speare's breadth of ability as she explores different areas of writing: contemporary how-to pieces, historically informative articles, and plays. They show her early and abiding interest in history and display her clear, often humorous writing style. Some themes that later develop more fully emerge for the first time in these shorter works. Although their significance may pale in comparison to that of the novels, they are important for their revelation of Speare's essential style and subjects.

3

Fact and Fiction: *Calico Captive*

Speare's first major attempt at writing demonstrated her gift for creating memorable characters, exciting plots, and vivid, realistic settings that transport the reader quickly into an earlier period. As was usually the case with her, a chance reading of a historical document sparked her imagination. Moreover, *Calico Captive* contained the first expression of Speare's abiding interest in moral values and strength of character exemplified most often but not exclusively by courage and loyalty. Family bonds, important in all of Speare's novels, are first explored here. She also exhibited a praiseworthy objectivity in her portrayals of religion and of Native Americans and their culture, an objectivity which was to continue in her later novels.

Research and Writing

Elizabeth Speare was the typically busy mother raising her children and tending to her family's needs until both Alden, Jr., and Mary were in junior high school and she had more time to herself. "Then one day I stumbled on a true story from New England history with a character who seemed to me an ideal heroine for a book for girls" (Booklet). While reading Walter Hard's *The*

Connecticut,[1] Speare became intrigued by a chapter titled "Mrs. Johnson Remembers," which outlined the story of the four-year Indian captivity of Susanna Johnson and her family. The events intrigued Speare, especially the references to a younger sister, Miriam Willard, and the "'spruce young spark'" (Hard, 125) who was the last to leave the family's party that fateful evening before the Indian attack. The brief account in Hard's book led Speare to seek out Johnson's diary, *The Narrative of the Captivity of Mrs. Johnson,* in its 1807 edition. The rather shadowy character of Miriam, Susanna's younger sister, fascinated Speare; there was plenty of leeway for wondering about the fourteen-year-old's thoughts and actions during the ordeal, and gradually Speare's imagination began to take over, to create adventures and to expand Miriam's characterization. Other characters and scenes began to develop from the narrative, but with all of this imaginative activity came the need for intensive research.

Speare's research for *Calico Captive* was typical of what she did for all her subsequent historical novels. Generally her delving into historical sources, combined with writing, takes one to one and a half years. "I don't think it takes a whole year of research before I start to do anything. I do a great deal of research first, and then I bring piles of books home to read in the evening while I'm writing during the daytime. I keep a pad of paper beside the typewriter to jot down questions: how long does it take to go from Saybrook to Wethersfield by boat, that sort of thing. Then I have to go back to look it up at the library so that I am constantly going back and forth. It took about a year and a half to do all the young people's books" (Interview). Regarding the writing of *Calico Captive,* she confessed, "I knew nothing at all about Montreal, and when they [the Indians and the captives] crossed the river, I had to do a good deal of research" (Interview). She was especially impressed with the Jesuits and how kind they were to the Indian children. Since Speare had never been to Montreal, she wrote to the city's chamber of commerce for information. Using this material and facts gleaned from other reading, she was able to recreate for the reader a sharp, lifelike picture of the sights, sounds, smells, and dangers of Montreal life during the 1750s.

The story opens with the guests leaving a party at the Johnson cabin in Charlestown, New Hampshire,[2] and with Phineas Whitney saying lingering goodbyes to Miriam Willard. Miriam is Susanna Johnson's fourteen-year-old sister who is living with Susanna, her husband, James, and their three children. Their happiness is short-lived, however, for an Indian raid early the next morning results in the captivity of the Johnson family, Miriam, and Peter Labaree (spelled Labarree in the diary).[3] The hardships of their forced trek to the Indian camp, their stay there, and then the journey to and the life in Montreal (among the French settlers, who are the Indians' allies in the war with the British settlers) are vividly portrayed and include Susanna's giving birth on the trail with Miriam's help. Their changing fortunes in the French city as they await the return of James Johnson with ransom money are depicted in detail; Miriam enjoys parties, pretty dresses, and the attentions of a handsome young Frenchman, leaving her with decisions to make about her future. In contrast, Susanna never loses sight of their captive circumstances despite all of the levity and finery surrounding them.

Since the protagonist, Miriam, was approximately the same age as Speare's daughter, Mary, Speare read the manuscript in progress to her to get her reactions. "Her encouragement kept me writing and her frank comments kept me strictly down to earth."[4] However, Speare also had her doubts, which were heightened by initial rejections of her early chapters by two publishers.[5] Then she sent the first three chapters to Mary Silva Cosgrave at Houghton Mifflin. Cosgrave, intrigued, acquired a copy of the captivity narrative, read it, and asked Speare for more of her work. That was the incentive that she needed to spur her on to finish the book. Speare's completed manuscript was then accepted, with suggestions for some revisions, by Houghton Mifflin. Cosgrave made the recommendations for changes, for she felt that "the last half of the book was not as well paced as the first half."[6] She also asked Speare, "Would it be possible to incorporate a brief explanation of the war situation somewhere in the story?" (Cosgrave 1), which Speare did through a conversation that Miriam has with James when they first catch sight of Montreal and

Miriam wants to know why there is not enough room for all people to live together peacefully (*CC,* 80–81).

Another difficulty that Cosgrave found with the original manuscript was that "it is puzzling to have her [Miriam] accepted by
the Governor's wife and permitted to attend the social functions
and be accepted like a guest instead of an enemy at the Du
Quesnes and allowed to go free while Susanna and her family are
imprisoned" (Cosgrave 1). Speare solved that problem by having
the imprisonment take place after James has belatedly returned
with a letter of credit. By that time Miriam is no longer staying
at the Du Quesnes as a guest. She has a small room of her own
from which she is doing her dressmaking. She was not imprisoned
because the paper that the soldiers have for making their arrests
specifies only the Johnson family. Earlier both Miriam and Susanna are accepted by the Du Quesnes because a tidy ransom is
expected.

One last hurdle was left for Speare to surmount. Miriam
chooses to marry Phineas at the end and leaves Montreal. Because Speare had presented a more sympathetic characterization
of Pierre in the original manuscript sent to her, Cosgrave felt that
Miriam should have stayed in Canada and married him "since
Miriam has now developed into a girl of spirit and character"
(Cosgrave, 1). However, that would be impossible if Speare remained true to the diary, for in it Miriam returned and married
Phineas Whitney. At first Speare "worked that into the first chapter, but it still wasn't convincing enough. All I could do was to go
back and cut Pierre down to size so that he was no match for
Phineas, so that he was a little bit more crude and a little bit more
selfish" (Interview). Then Miriam's choice at the end became
much more plausible.

Influence of Setting

Eudora Welty, in *Place in Fiction,* states repeatedly the importance of location in fiction. Although she was speaking of realistic
fiction, her own genre, rather than historical novels, her obser-

vations nevertheless apply to Speare's genre as well. She contends that "fiction depends for its life on place. Location is the crossroads of circumstance, the proving ground of 'What happened? Who's here? Who's coming?'—and that is the heart's field."[7] Furthermore, she maintains that "place has a good deal to do with making the characters real . . . and keeping them so" (Welty, n.p.). Welty's ideas are exemplified even in Speare's first novel, for Speare demonstrates from the start that she knows how to give her readers a strong sense of locale. Indeed, it is one of the best features of the novel. Margaret Sherwood Libby, writing for the *New York Herald Book Review,* stated that "it is that rarity in historical novels, one that does not seem to be written to provide 'background' but to tell a good story, in which the setting is important both because it affects the characters and plot and because it is vividly recreated by the author."[8]

As already mentioned, the book opens at the Johnson cabin. Initially the cabin, although rustic, is a happy place because of the successful party that has ended, with all of the guests gone but Phineas (in the Hard chapter and the diary he is unnamed) who is lingering with Miriam (also unnamed in the diary until page 22). Even then there are constant reminders of the Indian threat as Miriam warns Phineas that he should not walk alone to the fort and that he should hurry or the gate will be barred for the night, just as the cabin door is barred as soon as he leaves. Both the time (1754) and place are already beginning to have an effect on the characters, creating tension. In this opening chapter Speare has skillfully woven in some of the necessary background information related to that setting and to the behavior of the Indians toward the whites. She also describes the hot summer setting, in which the women are forced to retreat to the fort for safety while their husbands are out trading, the dust and heat seeping into the reader's bones as well as into the women with their confined, whining children. D. C. Muecke has stated that "a sense of irony involves not only the ability to see ironic contrasts but also the power to shape them in one's mind."[9] The reader becomes fearful for Phineas, yet the irony is that, although this fear is justified several hours later when the Indian raid occurs, the reader's concern has been misplaced: it is the Johnsons who are all taken prisoner, not Phineas. There is further irony when Miriam talks about how everything can change dramatically in one day, for she is thinking about Phineas and how his coming has changed her life, yet her words become prophetic in a more sinister fashion when the Indians burst into their cabin, and her life is again abruptly transformed.

Speare sticks closely to the diary with the events that precipitate the raid. The Indians lie in wait as Peter Labaree, a neighbor, comes to the Johnson cabin, where all are asleep; Labaree has come before dawn to get an early start on some work that he has promised to do for James Johnson. Labaree does not see the Indians who lie in ambush, and when the door is opened, they burst in after him and capture "Labaree and Mr. Johnson and one of the hired men and [rush] through the house" (Hard, 125). In the diary, another hired man living there manages to escape, sounding the alarm at the fort. In the novel, there are no hired men staying at the house; it is Miriam who tries to escape to run to the fort for help, but she is stopped by the sight of the frightened children looking at her, and when she tries to get them out the window instead, it is too late—they are all caught by the Indians. Miriam is taken along with Susanna and the three children, their naked state (mentioned in the diary) changed to a covering of shifts by Speare, who has the Indians grudgingly provide the captives with some of their own clothing for the march. Speare's changes serve to illuminate characters, increase tension, and sharpen the contrast between the warm, happy interior setting before the Indians come and the stark fear inside the cabin and on the trail once the Indians take the settlers captive.

The following terrors and difficulties of the trail, including the fast pace of the march, are intensified by Susanna's condition: she is expecting another baby soon, and the others fear that the Indians will kill her because she does not have the strength and endurance of the rest. Instead, the Indians have James, her husband, catch a neighbor's horse, Scoggins (who becomes "Scroggins" in Hard's account), for her to ride. That part is taken straight from the diary. Her three other children (Sylvanus, six;

little Susanna, four; and Polly, two), Miriam, and Peter Labaree are able to keep up. When Miriam helps deliver the infant (James is there, too, but remains in the background, almost nonexistent), Susanna names the baby Captive; later Miriam rescues the infant when Labaree, who has left behind a wife and three children (four in the diary), accidentally drops her into a stream while crossing. Not only does the trail present physical hazards and hardships, but one of the Indians, Mehkoa, becomes attracted to Miriam and pulls her hair and trips her to see what her reaction will be, adding to her difficulties.

Speare softens some of the true hardships on the trail in her novel, especially Susanna's account of her torturous ride on Scoggins's back: "Every step of the horse almost deprived me of my life" (Hastings, 29). When it became obvious to the Indians that she could no longer remain on the horse, "Mr. Johnson carried his wife in a sort of pack slung across his back. / Half starved and nearly dead from exposure and exhaustion, the party was met by the French at Crown Point" (Hard, 128–29). In the diary, Susanna relates that starvation was a real fear, too; the Indians finally killed Scoggins for food. That episode is glossed over in *Calico Captive,* but it has more prominence in the diary where the Indians offer "the prisoners the best parts of the horse" (Hastings, 32). Indeed, the children eat too much of it and are sick for several days. Also omitted from *Calico Captive* is the severe hardship that James especially underwent because, while barefoot like the others, he had the extra burden of carrying his wife on his back. Since the girls were usually carried by their captors, their feet were in better condition; however, in the diary (but not in the novel) they and Sylvanus were sick for a good part of the journey.

When they finally arrive in the Abenaki camp at St. Francis, they get an immediate taste of what life in their new setting will be like as Miriam gets switched walking the gauntlet and Labaree suffers a cut forehead when he falls. Because Miriam and Susanna are in different wigwams in the camp, as are James and the children, the reader gets to see much of what the place is like as Miriam goes to visit her sister and they meet others who pass by and share their news. Perhaps to the reader's surprise, Miriam is treated very well at first, assigned no tasks. When her inactivity becomes too boring, she asks if she can help sew designs on moccasins along with the other women in her wigwam, and they reluctantly agree. The situation changes abruptly when Miriam scorns Mehkoa's offer to make her his squaw, shaming him before his people; afterwards, no longer the favorite of the chief's son, she is treated harshly for the duration of her stay in the camp, and she finds out what a "no-good" squaw's life is like. She later discovers that unless she leaves with James and the two Johnson girls for Montreal where the Indians plan to sell them, she will be forced to become the squaw of an old Indian in the camp.

The Abenaki village setting enables Miriam and the reader to take stock of village Indian life and the Jesuit influence on them. The Jesuits have baptized many of the Indians. There is also a church in the village where prisoners and Indians can go to mass, although Susanna refuses another prisoner's invitation. According to the diary, the Indians' "attendance was pretty general" (Hastings, 71). The setting also reveals more of Miriam's character and her love for her sister, whom she does not want to leave. To a lesser degree the reader understands more about Susanna and her worries about her children; James has the smallest role here among the family members captured at the cabin.

When the scene shifts to Montreal, the reader sees everything through the astonished eyes of Miriam. She sees the streets and the marketplace filled with city sights and smells, and she discovers that the city is one of sharp contrasts: while the wealthy have astoundingly opulent houses and clothing, the less affluent typically have shabby dwellings and not enough food. To some degree, both Miriam and the reader become caught up in the opulence and the whirl of the city's social activities, as Miriam busies herself making ball gowns and receives the attentions of Pierre, who plies her with hot chocolate and other treats and takes her on outings. The darker side of Montreal life reemerges, however, when Miriam goes to visit the Johnsons in the city jail: she finds it cold, damp, dark, rat-infested, filthy, and pervaded by an overpowering stench. This squalor shows up starkly against the gay background of preparations for luxurious balls and May Day festivities. Such dramatic scene shifts serve as reminders—again, to both Miriam and the reader—that there is suffering as well as pleasure in the city and that amid it all one should not lose sight of basic moral values learned in childhood. Susanna, in contrast with Miriam, never forgets what they are doing in Montreal and how they got there. However, Speare helps the reader to realize that it is easier for Susanna to be more sober and conscious of their position because she is older, more mature, married, and separated by force from her children. The young and vivacious Miriam, moreover, is witnessing and becoming a part of a luxurious life with beautiful dresses and elaborate parties for the first time. For all of these reasons, the setting has much greater impact on Miriam than it does on her sister.

By placing her characters in different locations in Montreal, just as she did in the Abenaki village, Speare is able to reveal more about the city's residents, their life-styles, and the political background. First Miriam is introduced to the Du Quesne household with its opulent furnishings and the rich attire of its upstairs occupants. There she is treated as a servant by Madame Du Quesne until the woman learns that James has gone to procure ransom money; after that, both Miriam and Susanna find their status elevated.

In another scene, Miriam visits her niece Polly, who has been bought by the mayor and his wife and renamed Alphonsine. This glimpse into the mayor's household initially shows the reader a slightly hostile, wealthy Frenchwoman angry at Polly's outburst of tears prompted by Miriam's visit. Later, when Polly runs away, the basically kindhearted woman realizes that Polly will never be happy with her despite all of the amenities of her household and her own love for the child. That love prompts her to do what is best for Polly, and she returns the little girl to her mother (Polly had been a clinging child from the very beginning of the family's ordeal, unwilling to be separated even slightly from her mother on the trail). The situation of Miriam's niece demonstrates yet another aspect of their captivity: her clothing and surroundings show how kind and loving the two women are who have taken her in as their little girl. She stays with them happily.

Later, when Miriam and her sister are forced to leave wealthy Madame Du Quesne's house and are taken into Hortense's already crowded, humble cottage, they discover weeks afterward that they have been diminishing the family's meager food supply as well as creating trouble for Hortense and her family by their English presence. Because the French and Indian War is underway, France and England are enemies, and neighbors who have helped Hortense in the past now refuse to prepare the ground for planting as long as the two English women are there.

The reader also catches glimpses of other life-styles as Miriam goes on errands through the crowded streets of Montreal, not always in the best sections of the city. By showing the reader a variety of settings within Montreal itself, Speare brings the city and its occupants to multidimensional life.

Characterization: Past as Present

Milton Meltzer wrote that "to have a sense of history is to have a sense of one's own humanity, and without that, we are nothing. The writer of history can help the child appreciate the past as an account of human experience, experience shaped within an [sic] historical framework" (Meltzer, 89). Rosemary Sprague made the added observation that "in an age when psychiatry is plumbing the human psyche to the depths, endeavoring to discover in past traumata the reasons for present actions, it would seem only good sense that a historical novelist should explore into the past of a nation or a world, and by that same process, try to bring to light the reasons for the swift changes in our present world."[10] Speare shows the reader the possibilities of courage for a present-day child through her characterization of courageous, realistic people (both real and imagined) who lived centuries ago. In addition to bringing past settings to life, she is able to create believable protagonists who have many traits similar to teenagers today. Such similarities make it easier for the contemporary reader to identify with the characters and to note the resemblances between the past and the present.

Although not as fully developed as it is in her second novel, characterization in *Calico Captive* is more than adequate and shows great potential. One example of Speare's realistic characterization is Miriam's instinctive selfishness during the Indian raid, when she tries to climb out of the cabin window to save herself and go to the fort for help and when she later thinks that she could have gotten away if it had not been for the children. These reactions are consistent with how Miriam later wishes, while on the trail, that they could leave Susanna behind somewhere so that they could reach their destination quickly (*CC*, 40). The girl who mourns the loss of her pretty calico party dress later finds it easy to forget her sister's worries about her scattered children and missing husband as she gets caught up in Montreal's social life. In that setting and those circumstances, so different from her former life-style where she had no one her age to talk to, she even forgets about the war between the French and the British, and her memories of Phineas begin to fade somewhat as the much-sought-after, handsome Pierre takes more and more notice of her and she of him. A contemporary young girl could easily identify with Miriam's actions and feelings.

As has been observed, a sense of place permeates the novel; it "has the most delicate control over character, too: by confining character, it defines it" (Welty, n.p.). Speare shows in various settings that there is more to Miriam than the early revelations of superficiality and selfishness. She can rise to the occasions that the locales create; for example, she overcomes her own terror and helps her sister through childbirth on the trail, and later she shows instinctive courage when she plunges into the stream, even though she does not know how to swim, to rescue the infant Captive. The adverse setting seems to bring out the best in Miriam as obstacles and hardships are thrown in her path. She also insists at first that she will stay with Susanna when the time comes for some of them to leave the Indian camp, until she is given forceful reasons why it is imperative that she go. Later, in Montreal, she continues to show increasing signs of maturity, especially after she leaves the Du Quesne household; for example, she shows a newly developed generosity when she sews a sprigged-muslin wedding dress for her friend Hortense to wear, instead of making one for herself out of the special material she was able to get. Miriam also reveals how far she has come as she debates what kind of life she will choose to lead: one of wealth, prestige, and leisure as Pierre's bride in the "modern" city, or one of hard work and challenge with Phineas back home where life is still full of danger and toil.

Susanna's character shows less development in the novel, partly because she is more steadfast in her actions and attitudes than her younger sister. She is the stoic adult no matter where she is or what problems she faces, with only a couple of exceptions. She worries about her only son, Sylvanus, at the Indian camp, and she experiences some wavering of faith and increasing depression near the end of the novel when her husband, long overdue, has not returned to Montreal with their ransom money. Always prepared to do the right thing, she insists on staying behind with the Indians while exhorting the others, including her husband, to leave for Montreal. He will have a better chance there of seeing to their ransom, and she wants to wait for Sylvanus's return from hunting with the Indians.

Once in Montreal her demeanor continues to be above reproach as she endures the separation from her children who have been sold to others. The dismay she feels when six-year-old Sylvanus quickly becomes captivated by the free life of the Indian males and is given an Indian name seems to fade a little as other, more pressing and immediate cares arise. Daughter Susanna, for example, adapts all too well to life with the two French Catholic women who buy her in Montreal (the Johnsons are Puritans), another loss for her mother. Not until Susanna and Miriam share a rented room after leaving Hortense and her family does she fall gradually into depression as they wait for the return of her husband, who is months late with the ransom money. It is at this point in the novel that Susanna is most fully developed. Susanna does have the infant, Captive, and eventually Polly is returned to her, too, which raises her spirits. Throughout most of the rest of the novel, her characterization is slight compared to that of Miriam and of characters in Speare's later novels.

The other characters are even less well delineated. James is a stalwart figure trying to do his best for his family under the most trying circumstances. He is away for a good part of the novel. Madame Du Quesne remains a flat, one-dimensional, haughty woman very conscious of her social position but with a sharp eye for any personal benefits she might derive from others. Her daughter, Felicité, is a superficial, flighty, but friendly child who takes to Miriam until Miriam deprives her of one of her beaux; then, like a child who has had to give up a favorite toy to another, she immediately becomes angry and snubs Miriam. Even that does not last, however, for, child that she is, she eventually forgets her hurt feelings when Miriam's circumstances change, and when she is with Miriam again, she chatters away as if they had always been the best of friends.

Pierre is slightly more developed, for he is seen from several angles as Miriam hears about him from Felicité, his grandfather, and others. His actions and speech reveal a great deal about his character: although dashing, boastful, and much sought-after by the ladies, he is illiterate and is far more at home on voyages to secure furs for trade (sometimes for a year or more) than he is in Montreal. As his grandfather tells Miriam, "His true heart is always in the forest."[11] When Miriam learns that as his wife, although she will have his wealth, she will have to do without his company for long stretches of time, she is appalled; in her daydreams of him, she has always pictured herself adventuring in the woods with him. Finally, Hortense, a servant at the Du Quesne residence and soon Miriam's good, loyal, intelligent friend, is depicted as just that and little else.

Portrayals of Native Americans

Elizabeth Speare had an unsettling encounter about her character portrayal of one group. "I had a troublesome experience with the Indians. Just recently after many years this girl came to see me. She was part Indian and was working through the library taking out the children's books that had a derogatory image of the

Indians, and she begged me to take *Calico Captive* off the market. She said I had changed my whole attitude toward the Indian between that and writing *The Sign of the Beaver.* Well, I hadn't, because in *Calico Captive* the Indians were the bad guys; there was no way to change that. That was history" (Interview). Perhaps the young woman took affront at bits of description of Pierre. For example, at one point "Miriam could sense the same barely tamed savagery that had never let her relax when Mehkoa was near. Pierre was as unpredictable as an Indian" (*CC,* 202). Later, at another meeting with him, she observes: "Once again, in the darkness, his face reminded her of an Indian's. His eyes, glinting under lowered lids, looked reckless and crafty" (*CC,* 244). There are other examples.

Speare, however, is otherwise as objective as possible in portraying Native Americans. Their part in the French and Indian War is well known, such as their capturing settlers and selling them to the French, yet she depicts them from the beginning as being fair about many things, just as Susanna Johnson did in her diary. The little food they have on the trail is shared equally with their captives. Miriam's natural fear and loathing of them under the circumstances is offset in part by James's comment to her: "An Indian friend isn't a bad thing to have, Miriam. Indians have a sense of loyalty too" (*CC,* 38). When Miriam emerges from the stream after her attempt to save Captive from drowning, the Indians treat her kindly, with respect, offering her the choicest breast meat and lighting a fire to dry her clothing. She ponders about them: "They have treated us well, Miriam had to admit to herself. Nothing like those stories of what they do to prisoners" (*CC,* 49).

At the Indian camp she receives two kinds of treatment because of her status as a favorite of the chief's son. At first nothing is asked of her; in fact, as has already been mentioned, out of boredom she asks to work on decorating moccasins. After her public refusal of Mehkoa's offer of marriage, she becomes a drudge for the women of her wigwam, enduring kicks and other blows. A similar fate at the hands of peers often awaits a contemporary favorite child who falls from favor. It is at the camp that Miriam discovers that many Indians have converted to Catholicism. Later, during the canoe voyage to Montreal, she learns from James that the Indians were paid by the French to attack and scalp the English settlers. By the time Miriam reaches Montreal and has to undergo the stares and reactions of the French, she has come to realize that there can be worse people than Indians: "There's more than one way to run a gauntlet, she thought. At least the Indians give you a chance to run" (*CC*, 85). Much later when she catches sight of her nephew, Sylvanus, with a group of Indian boys and tries to get him to go to his mother with her, he struggles free from Pierre's grasp and runs away. When Miriam accuses Pierre of letting him go, Pierre tells her: "'He's living the best life a boy could have, and I would to heaven I could change places with him!'" (*CC*, 204). Miriam, calling the Indians "savages" (an attitude one would expect from someone living in her time, in her position), is appalled. These two contrasting views are presented throughout with the scales more heavily weighted toward the good features of Native American culture.

Universal Themes

Contemporary children need to realize that their attitudes and feelings are not theirs alone. They need to become aware of what difficulties others before them have coped with and suffered through, for in that process they can experience possibilities within themselves that might otherwise be overlooked. Courage, loyalty, love, and other themes expressed historically show children the potential for relying on the same values today, enabling children to cope with the myriad problems that they now encounter. The best historical fiction presents universal themes while telling an entertaining story and bringing history to life in a way that no textbooks can, enabling the reader to see that although times have changed and many years have passed, people were essentially the same then as they are now. A child who perceives that connection between past and present has more hope for the future.

In *Calico Captive* Speare demonstrates the enduring themes of courage, duty, loyalty, and love. Miriam has often displayed courage, but certainly Susanna does, too, in the face of circumstances designed to test her severely as her family is torn apart. Even the children, each in his or her own way, show strength of character in being able to adapt, as little Susanna and Sylvanus do, or in a determination not to accept what seems to be the inevitable, as in Polly's case. Duty and loyalty are integral parts of all the characters, although Miriam is distracted from time to time by her new surroundings in Montreal. Speare portrays people with feelings of family love, as in the many examples already given. Miriam overhears her sister and James quarreling for the first time at the Abenaki camp and soon learns the reason for it: Susanna is adamant in her insistence that she remain there while her husband, their children (except Sylvanus), and Miriam go to Montreal. Only when James and Miriam face the reality of the circumstances do they leave, but with very heavy hearts. All of James and Susanna's hopes are for the family's reunion, and even Miriam, despite lapses, recognizes the pull of family ties. These are lasting values, not just ones applicable to more than two centuries ago.

Other universal traits are fear, bravery despite fear (the truest kind of bravery), and the failings any contemporary child can relate to, such as Miriam's love for pretty things and for having fun. A young reader today can also readily imagine and accept Miriam's being captivated almost in spite of herself by the talked-about, handsome Pierre who pays her increasing attention and who is also among the wealthiest men in town (or will be when his grandfather dies). Although the absent Phineas is still remembered, Pierre, often on the scene, especially at propitious times, gains a strong hold on Miriam's affections, ultimately forcing her to choose between the two men.

War and Religion

Speare obviously tries to take special care to present objective views on war and religion. After hearing James's explanation about the reason for the war, an obviously English point of view, Miriam soon learns some of the French attitudes towards the war and the English, and later she and Susanna must leave Hortense's cottage to get a room for themselves because of French antagonism: "There's a powerful bad feeling against the English these days" (*CC*, 175). Nevertheless, Miriam, after her initial encounter with the French when she arrives in the canoe, finds them to be anything but enemies. Indeed, for the most part, the war plays an important narrative role but a minor thematic one, acting mainly as a catalyst for the family's capture by the Indians, their being taken to Montreal, and their being sold. Later, James is delayed in returning with the ransom because of the war. Earlier the French are confident that the war will end soon in their favor. As time passes and the war victories alternate between sides, the novel is concerned with the characters and with how they react to their shifting circumstances, some of them brought about by the war, rather than with the war itself. Miriam and Hortense, for example, who should be enemies with their English and French backgrounds, know that even though their husbands may be enemies, they will never be such because of the strong bond of friendship that has grown up between them.

Speare presents a variety of attitudes toward religions. Miriam is startled to see Indian girls wearing dresses and walking primly with nuns (who had made the dresses, according to Speare's research) in Montreal. She is even more surprised to learn that they go to the Catholic convent school where they are taught "to sing hymns and paint pictures and sew and embroider" (*CC*, 108). The reader might question what they will retain of such teachings or do with them when they return to the Indian camps and to the hard work required of them there. If they are not to return to the camps, then what does the future hold for them? The young reader is left to wonder.

Four-year-old Susanna quickly accepts Catholic doctrine, and despite the fact that "all her life she had been taught to despise this mysterious evil called Popery" (*CC*, 129), Miriam finds that she cannot contradict the child's new faith since little Susanna derives such comfort from it. "Somehow . . . she could not believe that a difference in belief should cause any child to feel lonely and afraid. It was a very new thought" (*CC*, 130). The reader, in turn, should realize through such events and comments that he, too, should be more open in his attitude toward the beliefs of others that are different from his own. Not that all of Speare's characters' remarks about Catholicism are positive. At the Indian camp when Miriam comments about the kindness in the priest's face, her sister, Susanna, retorts, "They burned Hugh Latimer at the stake in England. Does that sound kind?" (*CC*, 65). But such comments are rare and are soon offset by the larger number of positive remarks.

When asked if her objectivity about religion was deliberate or unconscious, Speare replied: "I don't think it's unconscious. I feel strongly about this. I was especially impressed in the *Jesuit Relations* by Parkman [Francis, the noted historian] when he spoke of the priests and [how] they had their instructions . . . and one of their instructions was to remove their boots in the Indian canoes. And I thought, how different from the English, because I'm sure the English would have stamped right into the canoes without a thought. . . . They were very kind to the Indian children. There were descriptions of the little Indian children going to church in their little red dresses which the nuns had made for them" (Interview). Mrs. Hastings's narrative certainly reveals a more biased outlook toward French Catholicism: "The blind superstition, which is inculcated by their monks and friars, doubtless, stifles, in some measure, the exertion of pity towards their enemies" (Hastings, 120).

Style: Language and Contrast

Throughout the book Speare's conversational style and original imagery carry the reader along. For example, one Sunday morning at the Indian camp Susanna and Miriam hear the sound of a church bell. "A scattering of white prisoners came by, bowing to the two English women like pathetic ghosts of decent churchgoers" (*CC*, 65). Some Indian words appear: some are explained, such as *nigawes,* which means "mother"; others, like those Mir-

iam has to learn (e.g. *Danna witchee natchepung*), are neither
translated nor pronounced. One of the Indian names, Sabbatis
(spelled "Sabatis" in the 1796 and 1814 diaries), is described in
Frank Speck's *Penobscot Man,*[12] a source book used by Speare in
The Sign of the Beaver later, as corresponding to Jean Baptiste.
There is a scattering of French once the setting changes to Montreal, especially when Miriam first arrives and she and Hortense
exchange meanings of words with each other (*le lit*—"bed"; *la
robe*—"dress"; etc.; *CC*, 91). Such exchanges continue throughout
their friendship. When Miriam meets and becomes friendly with
Felicité Du Quesne, a few more French words appear. A sem-
blance of earlier times is also established for the reader through
some of the other language Speare uses, such as contractions ('tis,
'twas, 'twould, and the like) that are no longer used in contemporary speech.

Another feature of Speare's style is her use of contrast throughout, beginning with the opening chapter where the happiness of
the party is quickly followed by the horrors of the Indian raid and
the characters' enforced march. Miriam finds the behavior of the
Indians on that march and in their camp quite different from the
stories she has heard about them; that difference is sharpened
when she arrives in Montreal and is greeted by rude stares. Also
in Montreal, when Miriam first goes out with Hortense to do the
marketing, she sees how different the bustling, lively city is from
their own crude town of Charlestown, New Hampshire. The ele-
gantly built homes in Montreal are quite a departure from the log
cabins Miriam remembers from Charlestown, and she marvels
also at the laughter and chatter that fills the Du Quesnes's
kitchen, quite different from the sober industriousness she experienced in the New Hampshire cabin. Religious differences have
already been mentioned. There is sharp contrast too between the
life-style of the wealthy Du Quesne family and that of their servant, Hortense, and the other poor that Miriam gets glimpses of
and eventually joins when she leaves Hortense's home. Finally,
Miriam becomes well aware of the contrast between the scholarly,
obviously reliable Phineas Whitney, who has written her about
his feelings for her and his plans and hopes for the future, and

the illiterate but savagely attractive Pierre Laroche, who also wants to marry her.

Frequent dialogue helps to reveal characters as the story unfolds, but in addition Speare uses descriptions very well, maintaining a good balance between the two. She brings the rigors of the trail, the Indian camp, and Montreal vividly to life for the reader through various sharply focused scenes, and she writes in a rather direct prose style in the third person. Her concentration is centered on Miriam throughout the story, making it easier for the young reader to identify with the protagonist and to become immersed in Miriam's adventures and dilemmas.

Of special interest is the epilogue, which answers some questions about the characters but at the same time whets the reader's appetite for more. In it Speare reveals that the ransomed Johnsons and Miriam returned to America by way of England. Yet in Hard's account "Mrs. Johnson, Polly and Captive came back to the Connecticut River valley. . . . [While] Mr. Johnson was redeemed the following year" (Hard, 129) and was reunited with his wife on New Year's Day, 1758. Hard makes no mention of Miriam and what became of her. In the novel, a year after they are finally settled once more in New Hampshire, Sylvanus is brought home, "a wild young savage who could brandish a tomahawk and bend a bow but who could not understand a word of English" (CC, 273). Little Susanna is also restored to the family, "a fine-mannered and fashionable young lady who could speak nothing but French" (CC, 273). Nothing more is said in the epilogue about how well either child is able to adapt to a new life-style. When asked what happened to Sylvanus in real life, Speare replied: "He came back, but he was restless. He never quite adjusted to the life back in New England" (Interview). Like True Son in Conrad Richter's novel The Light in the Forest,[13] Sylvanus found that he no longer fit in comfortably anywhere. According to Hard, "He spent his life as a fisherman in Walpole, New Hampshire. He was never able to give up the free habits of his Indian days" (Hard, 130). Little Susanna was better able to cope, even without knowing any English when she returned. She maintained a correspondence with the two French women (three in the diary) who had treated her like their own daughter. More recently, in 1976, to help commemorate the nation's bicentennial, the town of Reading, Vermont, decided to refurbish the little stone monument Susanna Johnson erected on the spot where Captive was born.[14] All of the family's descendants were invited, as well as Elizabeth George Speare. Even the governor of Vermont was there. As a memento of the occasion, Speare has a photograph of one of the descendants. "There was a little Susanna, six years old with red hair, and they took a picture of her standing by the monument" (Interview).

Fact and Fiction

Speare chose to make changes in some of the characters and events in the diary in order to strengthen her novel, to change its focus from Susanna's account to Miriam's. Speare also adds a piece about Miriam's having a birthday that no one remembers on the trail; Speare has Mehkoa give her the cherished blue dress on that particular day to replace the tatters she has on. The shift in focus also meant dropping the hired man Farnsworth from those captured and not having any hired help at the cabin to spread the alarm at the fort. Sylvanus's character is changed, too, from a frightened little boy in the diary to the cocky, easily adaptable child who becomes a pet of his captors and quickly assumes their ways. In the diary Labaree not only drops the baby in the stream but also rescues her. Having Miriam attempt the rescue, especially as a nonswimmer, sharpens her characterization.

At the Indian camp there are further changes. In the diary, each captive walks the gauntlet with his or her Indian master: "We expected a severe beating, before we got through, but were agreeably disappointed, when we found that each Indian only gave us a tap on the shoulder" (Hastings, 60–61). A few days after their arrival, James is taken to Montreal and sold; afterward the girls, Labaree, and Miriam follow the same route, but at different times (Hastings, 67). Speare makes a much more dramatic event out of the family's departure by having the two girls, Miriam, and James leave at once, creating a scene between husband (who does not want to go) and wife, and provoking an outburst of protest from Miriam who also does not want her sister to remain behind alone. These changes bring out more of the crucial characteristics of those involved. All of the episodes with Mehkoa at the camp were created by Speare. There was one young Indian, age 16, among the 11 on the trail, and he acted in the diary as Speare had Mehkoa act: "He often delighted, by tormenting my sister, by pulling her hair, treading on her gown, and numerous other boyish pranks, which were provoking and troublesome" (Hastings, 38). The diary gives no indication of Miriam's response to such torments. In the novel such a reaction is necessary, and Speare fuses the real and the imagined into purposeful episodes that not only reveal character but also provide an excuse for Miriam to leave hurriedly with the others when she wants to stay with her sister.

When the baby girl is delivered on the trail, she has no name in the diary until later in Montreal when she becomes very ill and the Du Quesnes want her baptized. Susanna acquiesces. Monsieur Du Quesne is the godfather, and his wife asks that the baby be named Louise after her. Susanna adds "Captive" as her middle name. In the novel, after the baby's birth Susanna simply states that she will be named Captive, very appropriate under the circumstances and more acceptable to readers who might wonder at a baby who goes unnamed for months. Speare distinguishes Polly by having her cry when her mother is out of her sight, which leads to her fictional inability to adapt to life with the mayor's wife and to run away, events not in the diary. Finally, in the diary as compared to the novel, Sylvanus is more frightened and less quick to adapt to life among the Indians: for example, in the diary he runs crying to his mother in the Indian camp when he learns he must go on a hunt, for he fears he will never see her again.

In connection with the times spent in jails, there are many divergences from the diary. In it James leaves a few days after Susanna is brought to Montreal. The month after his long-delayed return, he is put in prison until Susanna can talk to the governor. Upon his release he, Susanna, Polly, and Captive set sail for Quebec where their real imprisonment begins. Miriam is kept in Montreal even though her ransom is paid. Since reality does not always make the best fiction, Speare wisely chose to truncate the narrative and to move some of the Quebec jail scenes to Montreal. Because she created Pierre entirely from her imagination, she needed a variety of ways for him to be of service to Miriam, and helping Miriam visit the Johnsons in jail was one of them (grabbing Sylvanus was another).

Throughout the diary Miriam's name is only mentioned twice, once in the narrative and once in a footnote that tells readers that she later marries "the Reverend Mr. Whitney, of Shirley, Massachusetts" (Hastings, 132). Her superior skill as a seamstress is a Speare fabrication from a comment in the diary that both Susanna and Miriam will take up their needles when their money runs out. In the diary, Miriam continues to do needlework when she stays on in Montreal. Other touches, like the balls they attend and the maypole activities, do not specifically appear in the diary but most likely come from other sources. Certainly the real Susanna mentions that while they are waiting for James's return and he is not yet overdue, they attend parties, go out to dine at other homes frequently, go for carriage rides, and are treated very well, even given presents. Speare fills in these general comments with rich, detailed scenes that bring the story to life.

Although children can read and enjoy *Calico Captive* without having read Susanna Johnson's diary, adults should find the comparisons fascinating, for they give insights into the creative talents of the author and how she is able to convert historical fact into lively historical fiction. If some of the characters are diminished in the process, such as James Johnson, others (even if they are changed) emerge much more clearly as individuals, like Sylvanus. Deletions of characters, such as the hired hands (Farnsworth in particular) and one of the three Frenchwomen who buy Susanna, enhance and tighten rather than hurt the narrative, giving the reader fewer extraneous characters to keep track of. The additions of Felicité, Hortense, Pierre, and others create texture and more complexity, while changes in the Johnsons' situations in the Du Quesne household only partially mirror occurrences in the diary but give the author opportunities to reveal more of Miriam's personality and courage. Overall, then, Speare's choices in translating fact into fiction have proved to be apt, especially for a first novel. There are faults, but, as discussed below, they are relatively minor for a first attempt at full-length fiction.

Critical Reception

The book has some problems in its execution. As mentioned earlier, most characters are not as fully developed as they are in the next novel; only Miriam shows extensive development. The plot resolution is no surprise; some of the earlier situations are also too convenient, such as Miriam's astonishing dressmaking ability, Hortense's finding Miriam and Susanna when they have been forced to leave Madame Du Quesne's on short notice, and Pierre's frequently encountering Miriam on the street at crucial times. Vivian Scheinmann calls the narrative "leaden" with "an overdone interior monologue" and says that "the racist language used in describing the Indians is deplorable,"[15] an unjust accusation given the objectivity already described and the narrative point of view. One would not expect Miriam in the 1750s to have the more enlightened attitude of the late twentieth century. The original Scheinmann entry, by the way, gave an incorrect date for *Calico Captive,* citing the publication date as 1959 instead of 1957; the error was corrected in subsequent editions.

On the whole, however, the book has been well received by the critics who have praised characterization, plot, and the vivid writing. For example, the reviewer for the *Bulletin of the Children's Book Center* writes: "The author has drawn her characters with a deft touch and paints a vivid picture of the danger and difficulty of such an experience without ever resorting to sensationalism or melodrama."[16] Another reviewer in the *Junior Bookshelf* comments about Speare's successful use of "conflict, in the literary sense, between individuals rather than vague blocs. This helps to lend conviction to a story which must be among the most impressive of forgotten epics of everyday heroism."[17]

Writing historical fiction is like walking a tightrope, for the author must carefully balance the amount of research included in the novel so that it is not too meager nor too overwhelming. Speare has succeeded in maintaining that balance. Historical fiction must also be true to the facts. Speare mentioned that "there was a wonderful scene in Thomas Costain or somewhere of the fairs that they had on the shore of Montreal when the *coureurs* would come back with their flotilla of canoes, and the Indians and they would set up tents along the shore and trade their furs. . . . It was a holiday for the townspeople and they all turned out for this—special food and special banquets—and I had written a wonderful chapter about that" (Interview). When she wrote to the Montreal chamber of commerce to ask about such fairs, she found that they either did not exist at the time of her novel or had been discontinued, and so she had to remove that chapter.

Meltzer has said that history "can develop their [the young readers'] perception about the past. To have a sense of history is to have a sense of one's own humanity, and without that, we are nothing" (Meltzer, 89). The same is true for the good writer of historical fiction. *Calico Captive* was a promising beginning to what was to become a distinguished writing career that would help readers to see their own potential through the reading of absorbing stories about earlier times. The highly respected British historical novelist Rosemary Sutcliff wrote that "the prime object of writing an historical novel is an exercise of the *heart* rather than the head. It is an exploration of the imagination, a discovery of other people living at different times and faced with other problems than our own. In other words, it is an extension of the author's human sympathies."[18] In her first novel Elizabeth George Speare was able to take an actual event from the past, to incorporate her attitudes and beliefs through her created characters and their actions, and to combine those elements into a book set more than two centuries ago that can still speak directly to a young person of today.

4

Moral Issues:
The Witch of Blackbird Pond

For her second novel, Speare wanted a heroine as spirited as that of her first. She spent months reading her state's history for another spark of inspiration, but none came. Then one day, walking by a stream in Wethersfield with her husband, she imagined the presence of another figure, a solitary young woman. Slowly other characters began to take shape, and appropriately the setting became Wethersfield, the Connecticut town in which Speare had been living for 20 years and which was "one of the first Connecticut settlements. . . . I chose the year 1687 arbitrarily because the story of the Connecticut Charter was irresistible . . . revealing in miniature all of the powerful forces which . . . were moving America irrevocably toward independence" (*CLR*, 205).

Research and Writing

Further research turned up a true account of a wealthy young woman who went to Boston with 10 trunks to visit her grandmother and who wrote letters home complaining about conditions in Boston, such as having to drink water with meals instead of wine (Interview). Speare carried that situation a step further, imagining what such a person would have felt coming to an isolated, far more rural community like Wethersfield where life was much harder, where everyone had to work to contribute to the family well-being and to the community, and where religion played a major restrictive role (Interview). In the autobiographical booklet put out by Houghton Mifflin, Speare further recalls: "I was intrigued by an account from early New England history of English children who were sent from Barbadoes [*sic*] to Boston for an education. I wondered what would happen if a girl from that sunny and luxurious island had come not to Boston but to the small Puritan town of Wethersfield in 1685 [*sic*]" (Booklet).

Research continued, made easier because Speare lived in Wethersfield which "is almost a suburb of Hartford" (Interview), the state capitol. The noted British historical novelist, Hester Burton, wrote that "every novelist finds joy and an extension to his life in the characters which he creates in his stories, but the writer of historical fiction has yet another pleasure, which is his alone. It is the pleasure of discovery. The results of the research necessary before the writing of any historical novel open up for the author a new and absorbing world" (Burton, 302). In Speare's case her research led her to the basement of the State Library in Hartford. There Speare found "ancient ledgers in almost undecipherable old handwriting which recorded the testimony which was brought in to the ancient witchcraft trials" (Interview). The unbelievable, ridiculous testimony of "ignorant neighbors and sometimes downright spiteful neighbors . . . taken seriously by sensible, pious, godly folk" (Interview) is shocking now, but in the late seventeenth century 11 women were hanged for witchcraft in Connecticut, 3 of them in Wethersfield. Speare used some of the testimony verbatim in her second novel. She also had the restored Williams house, which had been the biggest house in Wethersfield, as a place to go to for her interior settings.[1]

Diligently and happily she continued her research to find out what people wore in the seventeenth century, what they ate, and how the food was prepared, to name just a few examples of the sort of information she needed. Speare has said that "I don't think that I deliberately planned it this way, but I found that a wonderful way to describe a scene is to have an alien describe it. I think I used that in almost every book" (Interview). It worked very well in *Calico Captive,* and it led to the creation of an exotic past for Kit, the name Speare chose for her main character because it sounded lively and spirited. Through such alien eyes scenes can appear fresh, full of many details that a native might easily take for granted and not even notice. It is also easier and quite logical for strangers to a region to make mistakes in behavior and in conversations in the unfamiliar settings and situations.

Speare had felt from the beginning that Kit was a lonely character who would need someone else—preferably lonely, too—to talk to and to confide in. Thus Hannah Tupper the Quaker was born. The other figures gradually emerged: "Two young men, one shy and uncertain, the other self-confident and merry. Behind them, shadowy, indistinct, other people waited" (*CLR,* 205). The setting for Hannah's isolated home and part of the title of the book came from a tiny spot on an old map labeled "Blackbird Pond" (*CLR,* 205). In addition to using real places, Speare mentioned that she tries to use real people in her novels whenever possible.

> Gershom Bulkeley in *The Witch* was a marvelous character. He was written up in Stiles's *History of Connecticut,* and he was exactly the way I tried to make him, opinionated, a very brilliant man, a doctor, a surgeon, a minister, and also a very arbitrary, dictatorial man. . . . I wondered how he would feel about witchcraft because he was a very brilliant and highly educated man, and I found in the Trinity College rare book room a little pamphlet written by Gershom Bulkeley on witchcraft. . . . He believed in witchcraft thoroughly because everybody did. There was no question in anybody's mind about this. He did say we had to be very careful. We had to not jump to conclusions. We had to weigh the evidence very carefully before we condemned a witch, which gave me the loophole for that trial [in *Witch*]. (Interview)

The writing process for *Witch* went much faster than for *Calico Captive* even though the second book was longer than the first and the characters more complex. "It was fun to write that one: I had a good time writing that. . . . I don't think I was writing for children. I was just writing a book. If I had an audience, it was a much older one than was reading *Calico Captive*" (Interview). Speare said that she had thought that the new novel would be for 12- to 13-year-olds rather than the younger readers now attracted to it. She sent the first four chapters to Cosgrave at Houghton Mifflin, who greeted the new work enthusiastically: "All of us here are thrilled with THE WITCH OF BLACKBIRD'S [*sic*] POND (a terrific title). . . . You have recreated the spirit of the times so magnificently that I found myself coming back to the present with a growing sense of unreality."[2] Cosgrave made only a few suggestions for minor corrections, saying that "we do look forward to publishing this book" (Cosgrave 2).

When the rest of the manuscript was received, Cosgrave wrote another glowing letter to Speare: "The witch is absolute perfection—a magnificent book!"[3] Again she made a very few minor suggestions before bringing up the subject of illustrations. "What would you think of not illustrating the book? The text is so vigorous it illustrates itself beautifully for the reader, and I fear another hand in this might give it a common denominator which it should never have. Besides, it is a novel which adults should read with pleasure also and text illustrations often pinpoint a book as a juvenile" (Cosgrave, 3). Apparently Speare agreed; her novel appeared with a mood-capturing painting on the book jacket by Nicholas Angelo depicting a young woman in the foreground, cape and hair blowing in the wind, standing at the edge of a meadow with a tiny figure and a cabin in the background. The endpapers in the first edition of the book were equally attractive, done in a bluish gray and focusing on the background section from the cover, the apparent figure of Hannah with a cat, heading for her cabin. The painted papers were dropped in later editions. Speare did not use an outline in the writing of this book, as she had for her first and would do for all of her others, including her adult novel.

Speare mentioned that "I know how I am going to end it [the novel]. I know when I start how it will end. People say they don't, they just go ahead, but I knew where I was coming out. I had no idea how" (Interview). Of course, with *Calico Captive* the historical record determined how that book would conclude. "That's the reason I wrote *The Witch;* I wanted to have a choice. I didn't want to be tied to history too much. I knew that Kit would be accused, but I had no idea what I would do about that" (Interview).

The Influence of Setting

Once again, Speare creates a strong setting with sufficient details to give it verisimilitude but not so many as to overwhelm the reader. Cosgrave wrote to her that "the period is so vividly real that we were right there every moment" (Letter 3). Speare has said that "I try to make it a rule that the historical facts or tidbits that I put in, play in some way toward the plot, add to or advance it in some way, or work into some necessity of the plot" (Interview). For that reason she had picked the particular year of the conflict with the Connecticut Charter, 1687, and chose a site she knew well. Eudora Welty stated that "when we write a novel out of the saturation of place, we have more to draw on than we know" (Welty, n.p.). The 20 years that Speare had lived in Wethersfield gave her a special kinship with the locale that research alone could not supply. Furthermore, "by concentrating on the sameness [of the past and present], one can gradually slip into what is different. The most important sameness, of course, is human nature. Men and women and children have always known happiness, felt terror, been angry, felt irritable, known despair. The emotions are the same; it is what evokes them that changes down the ages. Remembering our own everpresent [*sic*] terror of the nuclear bomb, it is not so impossible to imagine a seventeenth-century Puritan's terror of hell-fire" (Burton, 302). Speare certainly convinces the reader of the sincere feelings of her characters in that distant time.

The setting has a profound effect on Kit, for it is far different from what she has known. She must constantly adjust to Wethersfield and the Puritan beliefs of the people living there that control their actions. Welty has said that "place, to the writer at

work, is seen as a frame. Not an empty frame, a brimming one"
(Welty, n.p.). For Speare the frame has overflowed, restructuring
the entire picture: place permeates everything, influencing characters as well as plot. The drab confines of Wethersfield lead Kit
to take refuge whenever possible at Blackbird Pond, a haven for
the pressures that she feels from her environment. In that setting
she experiences a sense of peace and well-being even while knowing that she is not supposed to go there.

Both the time and the place of *The Witch of Blackbird Pond*
influence other characters as well as Kit. This overall effect occurs because of Speare's ability to render setting in such a vibrant
way that the reader immediately becomes caught up in it, along
with the characters, and can readily believe in the rightness of
the characters' reactions to it, especially Kit's. The stark, restricted environment of Wethersfield parallels the closed minds
of many of the inhabitants and the confining religious beliefs of
the Puritans, just as the open-meadow setting of Blackbird Pond
represents freedom of spirit and expression for Kit and for young
Prudence Cruff. Speare's technique in incorporating setting as a
principal player in the action of the plot was used in *Calico Captive.* She again includes contrast and makes use of the views of
the outsider or newcomer to the scene who sees more than a native would.

Contrast

The Witch of Blackbird Pond is a study in contrasts. From the
beginning there is the cultural clash between Kit's Barbados upbringing and Puritan Wethersfield.[4] Kit is going from Barbados
to Connecticut to live with her only relatives. Even before she
reaches her final destination after the long sea voyage, she encounters far different views from those she knew at home. At Saybrook, a first stop in America, Kit plunges into the water to
retrieve a child's dropped doll, much to the astonishment and dis-
approbation of the boat's occupants, for staying afloat was a sign
of witchcraft to many Puritans. The frigid water comes as a shock

to Kit, a marked contrast to the warm water of the Caribbean that she had been used to when swimming. Later, she tells John Holbrook, another passenger, that she has read the plays of "Dryden and Shakespeare and Otway,"[5] he is horrified and responds, "The proper use of reading is to improve our sinful nature, and to fill our minds with God's holy word" (*WBP*, 25). For the nonreligious Kit who had free use of her grandfather's extensive library, this is another surprise.

The settings are contrasted as Kit describes Barbados to John: "'Tis as civilized as England, with a famous town and fine streets and shops. My grandfather was one of the first plantation owners, with a grant from the King" (*WBP*, 12). She had grown up there "running free as the wind in a world filled with sunshine. The green palms, the warm turquoise ocean meant nothing to him [John]" (*WBP*, 19). Kit's memories of this childhood paradise heighten her dismay at the gray dreariness of the scene when they finally reach Wethersfield, "a narrow sandy stretch of shoreline, a few piles sunk in the river with rough planking for a platform" (*WBP*, 26). No town or houses are visible.

When Kit goes with her relatives, the Wood family, to her first Sabbath at the Meeting House, they come to a clearing after passing some houses, and Kit discovers that "'this is the town.' . . . There was not a single stone building or a shop in sight. The Meeting House stood in the center of the clearing, a square unpainted wooden structure, topped by a small turret" (*WBP*, 51). Nearby are the pillory, stocks, and whipping post. Kit also learns that the wealth she had always taken for granted in Barbados is rare in Wethersfield and surrounding areas; John Holbrook, for example, has had to give up his dream of going to Harvard because of a lack of funds. He will study with the Reverend Gershom Bulkeley at Wethersfield instead.

Kit remembers her mother's description of Aunt Rachel, her mother's sister, as laughing and beautiful, but John warns Kit that many years have passed since Rachel ran away with Matthew Wood to America, and she may be different from Kit's imaginings. When Kit first sees Aunt Rachel at the door of her house, Kit takes her for a servant. Only when Kit meets her cousin

Judith, one of Rachel's daughters, does she realize what Rachel must have looked like when Kit's mother last saw her. The harsh climate (physical and intellectual), hard work, and the passage of time have all taken their toll on Rachel.

Kit's clothing radiates bright color and style beside the plain homespun of her relatives. Her uncle is equally dismayed by the seven trunks she has brought with her: "They filled one entire end of the room" (*WBP*, 38). Later, he becomes furious when Kit gives her cousins and her aunt some of her clothing, and he orders that everything, except for the warm shawl given to the disabled Mercy, be returned. He calls the clothing "frippery" (*WBP*, 43), a word he repeats when he first sees Kit ready to attend church on the Sabbath. "Beside the plain blue homespun and white linen which modestly clothed Aunt Rachel and Judith, Kit's flowered silk gave her the look of some vivid tropical bird landed by mistake on a strange shore" (*WBP*, 51). The townspeople are equally astonished by her attire. More surprises are in store for Kit as she learns that there are two Sabbath services that she will have to attend each Sunday, even though in the past she and her grandfather had rarely gone to church.

There are also contrasting political views. Speare chose 1687, a politically volatile year in which there was famous controversy concerning the Connecticut Charter. This document had granted the people a great deal more freedom than the English had living in England under King James. According to Samuel Lucas in *Charters of the Old English Colonies in America,* Sir Edmund Andros, appointed governor of New England by the king, had come to Hartford to confiscate the charter, but he was thwarted when it mysteriously disappeared from the table of the suddenly darkened assembly room. "When Andros was deposed in 1689, the Charter reappeared from its concealment [in an elm tree]."[6]

Speare introduces the conflict between the Charterites and the king's men through Matthew Wood and Gershom Bulkeley: Matthew is for the freedom the charter grants, while Bulkeley favors the traditional laws of the monarchy. One of Matthew's earliest questions to Kit is, "Your grandfather was a King's man, I reckon?" (*WBP*, 38). When Kit replies in the affirmative and asks if all Americans are not king's men, Matthew leaves the room without replying. Political matters come to a head early when Bulkeley comes to dine. Bulkeley says that he hopes that Kit will keep her allegiance to the king. Matthew, offended, gives vent to his feelings: "'I am mistaken . . . because I do not favor buckling under to this new King's governor?' 'Governor Andros was appointed by King James. Massachusetts has recognized that.'[7] 'Well, we here in Connecticut will never recognize it—never! Do you think we have labored and sacrificed all these years to build up a free government only to hand it over now without a murmur?'" (*WBP,* 61). Bulkeley says that such talk leads to revolution, to which Matthew responds: "There are worse things than revolution!" (*WBP,* 61–62). His attitude toward political freedom adds another dimension to his character and widens the scope of the universal theme of freedom in the novel. Freedom is also what Kit yearns for; freedom is implicit, too, in Hannah's circumstances, for the old woman merely wants the right to be left alone to live and worship as she sees fit.

Much later in the novel the political issues are again raised, when Gov. Andros comes to Connecticut. Speare devotes chapter 15 to reactions to the governor's appearance and to the disappearance of the charter, which William Ashby, Kit's suitor, describes. Although "the Colony of Connecticut is annexed to Massachusetts" and Gershom Bulkeley "will be appointed a Justice of the Peace for his loyalty" (*WBP,* 161), the charter is safe from Andros's hands. Matthew tells Rachel, Kit, and Judith, "There are hard times ahead for Connecticut. But some day . . . we will bring our charter out of hiding and begin again, and we will show the world what it means to be free men" (*WBP,* 162).

To a lesser degree Speare contrasts life at sea with life on shore, mainly through the character of Nat Eaton, whose life is the sea and the ship *Dolphin.* His dream is to have a ketch of his own. Although homecomings are special to him, so is setting out to sea on a voyage. His mother—who often goes to sea, especially during the winter months—expresses her feelings to Kit about ship and shore: "'Tis a good life [at sea], and one of the best things about it is coming home in the springtime" (*WBP,* 4). She spends winters on the ship to escape the harsh New England winters; she spends summers on land so that she can enjoy her house and garden. Ironically, the relatively tiny confines of the ship often provide a sense of freedom and excitement because of the expanse of sky and ocean and the unpredictable temperament of both not to be found to the same degree on the wider spaces of land.

Religious Attitudes and Freedom

There is little religious freedom in Wethersfield in 1687, when the book opens, as Kit soon learns. The Puritan religion with its focus on death and damnation and its rigid rules is worlds apart from the freedom Kit had experienced in her life with her grandfather on Barbados. As Louis B. Wright states, "Religion was not merely a Sunday ritual; in the seventeenth century it was an enveloping influence seven days in the week" (Wright, 72). Kit's former life of freedom, leisure, and pretty, colorful dresses must now give way to a quieter demeanor, chores, and unadorned, neutral colors.

Religious intolerance is demonstrated by the townspeople's attitudes towards Hannah Tupper, the old, wise, gentle Quaker who lives by herself at Blackbird Pond and who has never harmed anyone. Nevertheless, the reader learns that most of the Wethersfield Puritans call Hannah a witch because her beliefs are different from theirs, and Hannah is made to suffer for it. As Wright observes, "Let no one imagine . . . that our ancestors came in search of 'religious toleration.' Toleration was a concept that few of them recognized or approved. . . . Once firmly in the saddle themselves, sects that had been persecuted in England became equally zealous to root out heretics from their own order" (Wright, 72–73). It is from this type of zealous persecution that Hannah suffers.

Quakers especially were an anathema to the Puritans. In Boston in the mid-1600s, "fearful of Quakers' entering the commonwealth, the General Court tightened the laws to make it a crime for shipmasters to bring them to Massachusetts or for other individuals to aid them. In 1658, the General Court ordered the death penalty for Quakers returning after banishment" (Wright, 82). In the novel those same prejudicial attitudes are contradicted by the harmless, warm character of Hannah, whom the reader comes to know through Nat Eaton, the ship captain's son, and Kit. Nat explains some Quaker beliefs to Kit and tells her of the harsh treatment Hannah has suffered because of those beliefs. Wright states that "when a dweller in the mid-twentieth century tries to project himself into the period of his colonial ancestors, one of his greatest difficulties is a comprehension of the pervasiveness of religion and its universal influence upon men, women, and children of the earlier age" (Wright, 72). Through Speare's fine writing, strong characterizations, and well-constructed plot, readers come to realize that there were differing views of the Quaker religion at that time, just as attitudes vary toward religions today; perhaps young people will give some thought to the religious bigotry they may have experienced, seen, or heard about during their own lifetimes.

Slavery and Freedom

Speare addresses the issue of slavery in this work primarily in regard to the transporting of blacks from their native Africa. Nat Eaton is appalled at slavery. When Kit tells him that her grandfather had "more than a hundred" (*WBP,* 26) to work the plantation, he makes her realize the conditions under which the slaves arrived in Barbados. Irate, he continues, "There are plenty of fine folk like you here in New England who'll pay a fat price for black flesh without asking any questions how it got here. If my father would consent to bring back just one load of slaves we would have had our new ketch by this summer. But we Eatons, we're almighty proud that our ship has a good honest stink of horses!" (*WBP,* 26). Although this issue does not surface again, the point is made: blacks should have their freedom as well as whites.

Although the idea of freedom for blacks was foreign to many colonists, the desire for greater freedom for whites was much more widespread. Much of the focus of colonial American history that students read is on events in Boston and other places in Massachusetts; events in *Witch* give readers an opportunity to see that many Connecticut colonists had equally strong views about freedom from English tyranny. As Nat Eaton says, "How can a king on a throne in England know what is best for them [people in Wethersfield]? A man's first loyalty is to the soil he stands on" (*WBP,* 118–19). He has also pointed out to Kit that "there are two sides to loyalty. . . . If the King respects our rights and keeps his word to us, then he will retain our loyalty. But if he revokes the laws he has made and tacks and comes about till the ship is on her beam ends, then finally we will be forced to cut the hawser" (*WBP,* 118). Speare's use of sailing imagery here is effective and natural, coming from Nat. Nat's words carry a special conviction: it seems his seagoing life has given him a particularly keen appreciation for personal freedom.

Themes

Courage is a major theme in all of Speare's novels. It is a quality often displayed by Miriam in *Calico Captive* and also by Kit in *The Witch of Blackbird Pond.* Her setting out alone for Wethersfield with no money and no arrangements made beforehand for her arrival and stay in Connecticut gives a hint of her independence and impetuosity mixed with courage. She has the strength of will to act when Mercy's position and her own as teachers are threatened, and the courage to run to Hannah at night to warn her of the approaching witchhunt and to get Hannah to safety by once more braving the cold New England water to fetch help. She also has the strength of character to refrain from mentioning Prudence's name at her witch trial to protect the child, even though the withholding of that information will probably mean that the verdict will go against Kit.

Young Prudence, the little girl whose doll Kit retrieved from the water at the beginning of the novel, also shows courage by visiting Hannah's cottage, a forbidden place, and by standing up for

Kit at the trial. She has blossomed from the cowering, abused child presented at the beginning to a fearless girl willing to speak up for her beloved teacher. Even her father, Goodman Cruff, shows bravery in the end, defying his shrewish wife because of his elation and pride over Prudence's literary accomplishments, much to the delight of all present. Nat, banished from Wethersfield for earlier misbehavior, nevertheless risks arrest to appear at Kit's trial with Prudence. Finally, the invalid, Mercy, displays a different kind of courage when she unselfishly gives up the man she loves without saying a word when she sees that her sister, Judith, wants him.

Love in its various forms is yet another theme throughout *Witch:* love of home (of Barbados for Kit), of family, of God, of freedom, and love between individuals and the convolutions such love can take. In her Laura Ingalls Wilder Award acceptance speech, Speare spoke of the importance of "the bond of the family" (*HB* 1989, 464) to her readers and to herself. She portrays this bond in *Witch* through the close-knit Wood family, which eventually includes Kit. When the townspeople tell Matthew that Kit is a witch, he is quick to reply: "Any man who slanders one of my family has me to reckon with!" (*WBP,* 166). Disabled Mercy is especially beloved in the Wood family. When she becomes seriously ill, Matthew overcomes his personal enmity and decides to fetch Gershom Bulkeley, a physician who is also a bitter political adversary. Just as Matthew is about to leave to find him, the reverend appears on his doorstep: he has heard how ill Mercy is, and his concern for her overrides his and Matthew's conflicting views. Dr. Bulkeley tries a new technique on Mercy, a hot poultice, and she recovers. Another kind of love, the love of God—tied to the fear of him—is also evident throughout the novel, as family members pray together, attend the Sabbath meetings, and follow the church teachings in their behavior. Of course, not everyone has the same views about God, as previously discussed, just as different groups and individuals have different ideas of freedom.

The various love relationships become intertwined as personalities unfold. William Ashby is smitten at first sight of Kit and later begins to court her. He even builds a fine house for her.

Judith "sets her cap" for John Holbrook, and although he is in love with Mercy, when he suddenly realizes that Judith thinks that he has been coming to the house to see her, he can say nothing to hurt her. "Such utter happiness and trust shone from those blue eyes that John faltered, and in that moment of hesitation he was lost" (*WBP*, 130). Mercy's love for John has already been noted. In the end, a series of crises resolves the incompatible couplings to the satisfaction of all concerned. These resolutions may seem rather pat in some ways, but in fact they arise naturally from the circumstances of the novel, consistent with the previous development of character and plot.

Style

In addition to contrast, Speare frequently uses foreshadowing as an element of style. Kit remembers belatedly, after jumping into the water to retrieve Prudence's doll, her grandfather's words cautioning her to think before acting, and both John Holbrook and Nat warn her about watching her actions in her new Puritan setting. In similar fashion John warns Kit that her Aunt Rachel might be quite different from the mental picture Kit has of her. Later, foreshadowing reveals that Kit will make repeated visits to Blackbird Pond and Hannah, while increasing references to witches and witchcraft build a sense of foreboding in the reader. Kit feels a sense of apprehension on the day of the husking bee when she realizes that William may ask her to be his wife. Although that prospect should make her feel glad—for as his wife she would have status, wealth, and all of the freedom that the community would allow—still she feels a "cold little lump of foreboding" (*WBP*, 136). After an idyllic afternoon with Prudence at Hannah's, Kit wonders, "Was there some premonition . . . that made that moment so poignant, some foreknowledge that this was the last afternoon the three would ever spend together in the small cottage?" (*WBP*, 175). These and other instances heighten the reader's anticipation of what is to come.

Repetition is yet another feature of Speare's style, one that was not added consciously. When asked about her use of repetition, Speare replied: "Well, I hadn't thought of that, hadn't thought of that at all. You do so many of these things subconsciously; you don't do them intentionally at all. . . . Children write to me that I'm always mentioning Nat's blue eyes, and I was unconscious of this" (Interview). Throughout the novel, Kit's impatience and impetuosity are stressed. A sign of her growing maturity is when she is able to begin to curb both, which takes most of the novel. Her curiosity is also frequently mentioned and leads to her getting to know Hannah. The repeated references to witches and witchcraft have already been noted, building to the climax of Kit's imprisonment and trial for witchcraft. This particular element of style not only adds to characterization but also creates an interest in the plot development and unifies the novel.

Critical Reception

The Witch of Blackbird Pond was almost universally acclaimed by critics when it was published, evidenced by the Newbery Medal it received. Nevertheless, a few critics have found minor flaws. One criticism is based on a feminist view that "the book is marred only by the plot's revolving around the standard question: 'Whom shall Kit marry?'"[8] Since that was an all-important question for young women of the colonial period, its appearance in *Witch* may be considered part of the novel's authenticity rather than a fault. Also, that criticism is far from unanimous: for instance, Speare's novel is included in Adell and Klein's *Guide to Non-sexist Children's Books*.[9]

In *Notes from a Different Drummer*, Barbara H. Baskin and Karen H. Harris take issue with the portrayal of Mercy: "Mercy's characterization is simultaneously highly idealized and taken for granted. . . . Being both female and crippled, her qualities of forbearance, self-effacement, and unassertiveness are thereby multiplied. Where others are shown having a spectrum of personality attributes, Mercy is shown in extremes—it is she who becomes the most ill from the epidemic; it is she who is 'good enough' for the minister."[10] The annotation continues, with faint praise: "The setting of colonial America adds some mild interest to this typical adolescent historical romance" (Baskin and Harris, 305).

Apart from the rare lukewarm appraisal, the majority of critics obviously felt that Speare had achieved her goals. The consensus is perhaps best expressed by Margaret Libby: "Rarely has a book taken us back into seventeenth-century life as this does. The secret perhaps is that Kit is a fully realized character and so are her two cousins and the three young men who play important parts in the story."[11] All of the research and the writing have come together to present to the young reader a vivid picture of earlier times and the influence of those times on sharply realistic characters. Speare has said, in her Laura Ingalls Wilder Award acceptance speech, "I do not believe that a historical novel should gloss over the pain and the ugliness" (*HB* 1989, 464). At the same time, she feels strongly "that the hero with whom a young reader identifies should on the last page not be left in despair, but should still be standing with the strength to go on to whatever the future may hold" (*HB* 1989, 464). The reader of *The Witch of Blackbird Pond* can see the possibility of a bright future for Kit and Nat. In addition, as Jean Fritz writes, "the capability of responding to the past emotionally—with tears, laughter, pain, sympathy—surely increases one's appetite for life and helps bring the landscape of human behavior into clearer focus" (Fritz, 86). Because of the qualities the characters demonstrate that can also apply to contemporary people and their circumstances, young readers of *The Witch of Blackbird Pond* can sense the potential for independence and achievement for themselves as well as for the historical colonial characters. They, too, can have courage, loyalty, and love of family, values that never lose their significance.

5

Making Jesus a Person:
The Bronze Bow

> He trains my hands for war, so that my arms can bend a bow of bronze.
>
> *(The Bronze Bow, 87)*

A few years were to pass before the public was to get more writing from Elizabeth Speare. In 1961 she published two very different books—a small work of nonfiction, *Child Life in New England, 1790–1840,* discussed in Chapter 7, and *The Bronze Bow,* a historical novel set in Palestine. Although the latter book's Palestinian setting is a departure from Speare's earlier and later work, many of the themes and stylistic elements are not.[1]

Speare moved her setting to Palestine in this Newbery Medal–winning work for a specific reason: to portray a more human Jesus for children. "I never intended that book to be a public-school book—I never dreamed it would be," she says. "I wrote it as a Sunday-school supplement. . . . I thought it would be something Sunday-school children could read which would bring the era alive, and bring Jesus alive a little bit" (Interview). She disliked the portrayals of Jesus prevalent at that time both in books and in the media. For example, while she was working on the novel, there was "a radio show on, 'The Greatest Story Ever Told,' and whenever Jesus spoke, they would drop the voice two octaves"

(Interview). At the same time "they had a movie in which Jesus was just a white light on the hillside, and this is ridiculous for Sunday-school students. I wanted to make Him a person" (Interview).

Speare wanted that and more for her students. "I wanted to give my pupils, and others like them, a glimpse of the divided and turbulent society of Palestine, an occupied country with many parallels in our own day. And I wanted to stir in them some personal sharing of what must have been the response of boys and girls who actually saw and heard the carpenter from Nazareth" (*CLR*, 208). She began her research to authenticate the setting as well as the times so as to learn more about Jesus and the setting in which he lived. She read Jewish history; travel accounts with rich descriptions of locales, events, and people; Bible scholarship; and biographies of Jesus. Finally, she realized that her reading must end and the writing begin. She says that "research was defeating my purpose and only clouding my vision" (*CLR*, 209) about Jesus.

Speare started with a theme—the theme of the hero—instead of with characters as she had in her first two books. She wanted her pupils to "see that the preacher who walked the hills of Galilee was not a mythical figure, but a compelling and dynamic leader, a hero to whom a boy in any age would gladly offer all his loyalty" (*CLR*, 209). This preoccupation with theme was a problem, however, for she had no other characters to work with. Nevertheless, she started to write, beginning with a girl protagonist as she had with her two earlier novels until she realized that "Palestine was an eastern country in which women stayed submissively at home" (*CLR*, 209). She decided that she would have to use far too many unconvincing plot contrivances if she kept a heroine as the protagonist. One more false start occurred before the character of Daniel finally emerged, and even then he turned out to be far different from what she had at first imagined him to be: "He was to be the romantic and bold young leader of a band of Zealots." Instead, "this boy was unsure and defiant and bitterly unhappy. . . . I had a person at last . . . and to my dismay he was a wild and difficult one" (*CLR*, 209).

The book opens in Palestine at the time of Jesus, during the Roman occupation. Daniel, age 18, fled from his village to the hill caves five years earlier because of mistreatment by the blacksmith to whom he was apprenticed. He is filled with hatred for the Roman usurpers who killed his parents (his mother indirectly) and caused the mental breakdown of his sister. His only aim in life is vengeance; eventually he believes that Rosh, the leader of the robber gang in the hills with whom he has been living, is the Messiah who will one day lead a revolt against the hated tyrants. Later, persuaded at first by others and then finally moved by the words and actions of Jesus himself as compared with those of Rosh, Daniel comes to realize that the real power on earth is that professed not by Rosh, but by Jesus: not hatred, but love.

Characterization

The characters in *The Bronze Bow* are less well defined within themselves, less complex, than Kit in *The Witch of Blackbird Pond*. Speare relies heavily on repeating a few characteristics to reveal Daniel's feelings, such as Daniel's scowling and his hatred. The constant refrain of the two words begins on the first page: "Remembering, he scowled up against the hot noonday sun" (*Bow*, 1). His hatred is for the Romans and for all of the misery they have brought to himself and to others. His father and his uncle, along with four others, had been crucified; his mother had died a few weeks later, after staying with her husband for the two days and nights that he survived on the cross. That was when Daniel made his vow that "I would pay them back with my whole life. That I would hate them and fight them and kill them. That's all I live for" (*BB*, 82–83). Leah, his sister who was only five at the time, made her way to the crosses and was never the same afterwards.

Daniel's anger and distrust dominate the novel until Joel and his twin sister, Malthace (Thacia), enter his life and begin to show him the value of friendship and, eventually, of love. Nevertheless, despite this friendship, throughout most of the novel Daniel continues to scowl and glare, even when he speaks with Jesus who tells him that "hate is the enemy" (*BB*, 224). His hatred causes Leah to become desperately ill, yet he persists in nursing it, telling the Roman soldier, Marcus, who wants to say good-bye to Leah, "If you could save my sister's life, I would not profane our house. . . . I would rather let her die" (*BB*, 251). Only through the personal visit of Jesus does she recover. At that same time Jesus "looked deep into the boy's [eyes] and saw the bitterness and the hatred and the betrayed hopes and the loneliness" (*BB*, 252).

Leah's character is similar to Mercy's in *The Witch of Blackbird Pond:* both are portrayed as primarily one-dimensional; and both are disabled, one physically and the other emotionally. Yet Mercy, despite her physical weakness and limitations, seems the stronger of the two, since she is willing to give up the man she loves to her sister. Leah does not have that kind of emotional strength and succumbs to illness again (both emotional and physical) at her brother's reaction to her interest in Marcus, the Roman soldier who had been coming to see her without Daniel's knowledge. Leah is a fragile personality, crushed by the deaths of her parents and the sight of the crucifixions. Since these experiences she has never left the house nor seen any visitors, but she is brought out of her shell very slowly, first by Daniel's presence, then by Malthace's, until she is able to respond to the gentleness and homesickness of the young Marcus. Throughout most of the novel she is a cowering, frightened figure. Her frailty provides a sharp contrast to Daniel's anger and strength.

Joel and Malthace, the twins from a wealthy family, are more forcefully drawn. In particular, Malthace has a strong sense of self-worth rather than the typical self-effacement found in the women that Daniel has known: for example, when they share a meal on the hillside, she "made three small piles, equal piles, he noticed, not skimping herself the way his mother used to do" (*BB*, 6). Although the setting places limitations on her activities, Thacia is as independent as the times will allow and even crosses those boundaries on occasion, such as when she masquerades as her brother. She also has a great deal of empathy for others. Joel seems almost a contemporary figure, with his eagerness for adventure and his willingness to help the cause, but he also suffers from guilt, knowing his father's more traditional attitudes and hopes for him. Both Thacia and Joel, who had earlier begun to think, like Daniel, that Rosh might be the Messiah, come to believe in the preacher from Nazareth instead, well before Daniel can accept him on faith.

Rosh, the robber leader, has flaws that are obvious to the twins and to the reader long before Daniel realizes them. Rosh focuses on hatred, not love, as he seeks to destroy the Romans, and he has ulterior motives of power and greed as well. He does not hesitate to use people for his own ends, even if that means putting them in jeopardy. Rosh also is very changeable in his moods and quick to anger, both of which are hardly messianic traits. Early in the book when Daniel is recovering from a spear wound with Thacia's help and he tells her that he believes that Rosh is the Messiah, her response is to call Rosh an outlaw, an unlikely choice for God to make. Daniel begins to have doubts: "Rosh looked at a man and saw a thing to be used, like a tool or a weapon. Jesus looked and saw a child of God" (*BB*, 111). Eventually, Daniel sees Rosh for what he is.

Simon the Zealot—who, like Daniel, was once apprenticed to the notoriously cruel blacksmith, Amalek—serves as a foil for Daniel. He tells Daniel that Amalek is dead and that Daniel can return to the village. Simon turns his house and smithy over to Daniel and Leah, with one provision: Daniel must serve any legionaries promptly and courteously. In the meantime, Simon plans to follow Jesus. It is Simon who tells Daniel about Jesus, who prevails upon him to go to listen to Jesus speak, who tells him that there are other ways besides Rosh's to defeat the Romans. Simon says that he felt differently about the Romans before he heard the carpenter preach; however, the reader gets no real sense of his earlier attitude and change of heart. While he is persuasive in his arguments about Jesus, he remains essentially an undeveloped character.

A more unusual character is Samson, the huge, mute black man rescued by the robber gang. He devotes himself to Daniel after Daniel removes his chains through painstaking effort. Samson's loyalty throughout—demonstrated by his willingness to follow Daniel, even against Daniel's wishes when he believes that there may be trouble, and to risk his life for him—shows the power of love.[2] His selflessness later leads to his capture and apparent death. A newly married young man, Nathan, one of Joel and Daniel's recruits for Rosh, is also killed in the same foray in which Samson is captured, and Daniel begins to realize the heavy price of hatred.

Finally, there is Jesus himself. Speare felt that "in my portrait of Jesus I failed. . . . I wish that I could have climbed higher" (*CLR*, 209). He is too removed from the people and events surrounding him in the novel to appear any other way; he "remains a shadowy figure" (*CLR*, 209). The reader mainly sees him through the eyes of others who tell Daniel about him; Daniel's personal encounters with the carpenter are few. Also, those few encounters show only the loving, compassionate side of Jesus and none of his righteous anger and sterner moments. Because of his one-sided nature of extreme goodness and understanding in these scenes, he does not appear fully human. Tiredness is the only human weakness apparent in him. Nevertheless, many critics were taken with the portrayal. Margaret Libby wrote in the *New York Herald Tribune* that "the introduction of Jesus is done with such skill that He is neither diminished nor sentimentalized, a difficult achievement."[3]

Themes and Moral Issues

Moral issues are raised through the themes of the book, the primary theme being that of hatred versus love, which has already been documented. The title of the book comes from *The Song of David,* six lines of which Speare includes together in the story:

—God is my strong refuge,
   and has made my way safe.

He made my feet like hinds' feet,
    and set me secure on the heights.
He trains my hands for war,
    so that my arms can bend a bow
of bronze."   (*BB*, 87)

Thacia explains these lines thus: "when God strengthens us we can do something that seems impossible" (*BB*, 87). References to the bronze bow crop up frequently after that, and at the end Daniel comes to realize that "only love could bend the bow of bronze" (*BB*, 252).

Throughout the novel, the needs for faith and especially for patience are stressed, particularly in connection with Daniel. His lack of patience is shown repeatedly as the novel progresses—with Rosh, with Leah at times, with his work as a silversmith. Joel's father tells him, "We have need of patriotism like yours. But we have need also of patience" (*BB*, 67). Jesus, too, speaks of the need for patience while preaching about the importance of kindness and love. Later Simon tells Daniel about the healings that have occurred in people who have faith in Jesus. In the end Daniel accepts that faith, too: "We have to choose, not knowing. / To know Jesus would be enough. / Almost with the thought the terrible weight was gone" (*BB*, 252). Through that acceptance his psychological healing process begins, which parallels Leah's restoration to physical and mental health. His catharsis is like that of Matathias in the earlier play, *The Stranger*, although here richer plot and character development make the climax and denouement more acceptable and believable.

Speare has used patience as a theme in her previous novels; her heroes and heroines strive for it, and ultimately it becomes a sign of their new maturity. Sixteen-year-old Kit in particular has to curb her impatience and impetuosity in *The Witch of Blackbird Pond;* both she and Daniel are shaped by events that happen before the novels begin. Kit is the lively, freedom-loving product of her life on Barbados, while Daniel's psyche has been seared and twisted by the situations that destroyed his once-happy family and led him into bondage and mistreatment. Each must acquire patience for very different sets of circumstances but for the same reason: to show their adult capabilities and status.

An important moral issue has also been raised in regard not to the characters but to the book as a whole. Speare explains that *The Bronze Bow* has "been attacked as anti-Semitic so that it is not used in the schools very much—it is used occasionally. . . . I didn't have that feeling [of anti-Semitism]. . . . I was over-whelmed with the wonderful history of the Jewish people which I read extensively. It's such a marvelous history, I can't imagine how they would read this into it. But they did" (Interview). Apparently the objections came because of the perceived Christian bias: Daniel cannot find solace and love within his own Jewish faith, and both Joel and Thacia are quick to leave the Jewish teachings of their family and religion and accept Jesus as the Messiah. For example, at one point Joel disregards the Jewish law to wash before eating because of what Jesus has said. The same acceptance of Jesus' words and teachings is true for most of the other Jewish characters in the novel. Of course, since the coming of the Messiah is part of Jewish teaching, there is an argument for the characters' acceptance of Jesus as the Messiah. Nevertheless, Speare's novel gives the reader little sense of the debate that raged about Jesus in his own time and the number of Jews who did not believe that he was the one the Jews were waiting for. This one-sided approach to the subject may have prompted the charges of anti-Semitism. Herbert J. Muller, in his book *The Uses of the Past,* writes: "One cannot reasonably take for granted the certain truth of an exclusive divine revelation: a revelation that was granted to an obscure group at a particular moment in history, that was recorded by fallible men in narratives marked by manifest inconsistencies, that cannot be proved by independent reason, and that Christians themselves have never been able to agree upon."[4] Those who agree with Muller or who feel that the Messiah has not yet come to the Jews might therefore take exception, as Jason Epstein does, to "the smugness of its [*The Bronze Bow*'s] doctrine."[5]

Other complaints about the book arise from the era of the book's publication and what was happening in our country during that period of growing unrest and dissatisfaction with our government. "It came out in the sixties, and it was attacked because Daniel succumbed to the status quo in the end which I don't think he did. But he settled for giving up the violent fight. That book has been taken up in recent years by the Christian schools" (Interview).

Style and Substance: Contrast and Objectivity

Speare's style in *The Bronze Bow* is similar in many ways to her writing in *The Witch of Blackbird Pond;* in fact, the two novels are more similar than their disparate settings and characterization would suggest. One of her most prominent stylistic devices, repetition, has already been discussed. When asked about it in reference to *Witch,* she replied, "It was probably just carelessness in re-writing and editing" (Interview). In contrast, as mentioned earlier, her use of repetition in *The Bronze Bow* appears to have been more deliberate. Other features of her style discussed here— contrast and objectivity—will reveal more similarities to her earlier writing and will reveal once again how Speare heightens thematic substance through stylistic devices.

Contrast has consistently been a prominent feature of Speare's work, and *The Bronze Bow* is no exception. The confinement of his grandmother's shabby hut with its dirt floor weighs heavily upon Daniel in comparison with the freedom he feels in the robber caves in the mountains. By the same token the village seems small, poor, and dismal in contrast to the city of Capernaum, a harbor town with its splendid homes, its activity and bustle, its various colors and smells, myriad boats, and a multitude of fruits and vegetables in its marketplace. There Daniel enters Thacia and Joel's home with its tiled corridors, flowered courtyard, and many rooms, worlds away from his grandmother's village hut with its semidivided room. His rough manners also sharply contrast with Joel's father's formal behavior at the table.

The contrasting qualities of Rosh and Jesus have already been discussed, and they diverge more and more as the book progresses. There are other examples of contrast: for example, the simple meal with Jesus and the warm feeling of closeness surrounding it, compared with the feast of mutton Samson provides on the mountain that arouses Rosh's animosity and makes Daniel realize how uncaring the robber group is (except for Samson). There is also the more general comparison of the wealthy versus the poor. In most instances Speare describes a new scene or place through the eyes of an alien, such as when Daniel goes to Capernaum and sees both the city and the wealth of homes like Joel's for the first time, observing features that someone used to either environment might take for granted. The naiveté and idealism of the group Daniel and Joel gather around them are also in contrast to the attitude and demeanor of the man they are taking their orders from, Rosh. Some other contrasts emerge more gradually: for instance, Simon the Zealot, initially as violently and ruthlessly opposed to the Romans as Rosh is, comes to believe in the use of very different methods to combat them.

As in her earlier books, Speare tries to be objective in her portrayals of all characters. The hated Roman soldiers, often revealed in a poor light when there are several of them together, take on a different aspect when looked at individually. This difference is best shown by Marcus, the young soldier who comes to talk to Leah without Daniel's knowledge. Through the presentation of Marcus's character, the reader suddenly sees that some of the hated soldiers are young men of Joel's age who come from villages that were also invaded by Romans and who show obvious signs of homesickness. Such objectivity lends more credence to Speare's story.

Critical Reception

The Bronze Bow offers a contrast in criticism. Although it won a second Newbery Medal for Elizabeth Speare and was highly regarded by most reviewers, the book disappointed some readers. In the essay on Speare's work in *Twentieth Century Children's Writers, The Bronze Bow* is called "a tedious piece of work. . . .

Although the message is laudable, children will find the density of this book an overwhelming obstacle" (Scheinmann, 1156). Jason Epstein, in his essay "'Good Bunnies Always Obey,'" offers even harsher criticism, calling the book "thickly pious" with a "factitious historical setting," the language "drab and abstract," and, as stated earlier, its doctrine "smug" (Epstein, 80). He finally goes a bit far when he says that the Nancy Drew and Tom Swift books are superior—such a comment is hardly likely to lend credence to his criticisms.

It is possible that relationships in the novel might work better if the characters were more fully developed. The repeated description of Daniel as broad-shouldered, scowling, glaring, and full of hatred wears a little thin for this reader, getting in the way of and almost obscuring his other traits. Nevertheless, such criticisms are far outweighed by the praise.

Although *The Bronze Bow* does not have the wide appeal of the *The Witch of Blackbird Pond,* it nonetheless possesses many worthwhile features, including strong themes and plenty of action. Speare says, "It was used quite extensively for a time. And it was used in high schools. I was on a program in Stamford run by the students in Stamford High School. . . . They discussed *The Bronze Bow* and invited me to come down and discuss it with them. Then I got the Newbery for children's literature, and it was dropped [from high schools]" (Interview). Obviously the highschool students no longer wanted to read something that was thought of as a children's book. As I pointed out in the preface, however, some "best book" listings have even included *The Bronze Bow* while omitting *The Witch of Blackbird Pond.* Paperback publications of *The Bronze Bow* have further increased its audience.

Although Speare had to rely on research to create her settings in the book, when she eventually got to Palestine and went to the locales she used in the novel, "I was surprised to find how close my guesses had been" (Letter 1). Spear had done a lot of work with travel books, studying them to get the right feel for her settings. After seeing Capernaum during her trip to Palestine, "I don't think that I would have changed anything" (Telephone conversation). The hills in the distance seen from the city looked as though they could have caves in them (Telephone conversation). Anyone familiar with Speare's painstaking research will not be surprised that the imagined settings almost mirror the real ones, for she has a special talent for making places come to life. The same vividness was apparent in *Calico Captive,* in her presentation of the life and scenes of Montreal, another place she had never visited.

6

Robinson Crusoe Revisited:
The Sign of the Beaver

More than two decades elapsed before the publication of Speare's fourth historical novel for young people, *The Sign of the Beaver,* greeted warmly by most critics and selected as a Newbery Honor Book. The idea for the novel had been at the back of Speare's mind for a long time but needed the right impetus for her to do the necessary research.

This novel, like her first two, was the result of Speare's happening upon the real account of the difficulties encountered by a boy living in a wilderness cabin in Maine while waiting for his family to return. Theophilus Sargent was 14 when he and his father set out from Methuen, Massachusetts, in May 1802 to make a home in the wilderness north of Bangor in what is now the town of Milo, Maine.[1] Once the two-room cabin was built and the garden planted, the father left to get the rest of the family. Unfortunately, "he found the family sick with typhus fever" (Smith, 264) and had to delay their return to Maine until they were fit enough to make the long journey. There was no way that he could notify Theophilus of the change in plans. In the meantime, the boy was getting along quite well—until he grew careless about shutting the cabin door and a bear got into the cabin and destroyed his food supplies. "Luckily there was a friendly tribe of Indians in the forest nearby getting bark for canoe building. The chief . . . took pity on him. He left his son, Ateon Oseon, with him and generously provided for the two boys until Theophilus' family finally arrived just before the river froze" (Smith, 264).

Speare recalls that "what had immediately fired my imagination was the relationship between the white boy and the Indian. . . . How would two boys from such totally different worlds appear to each other? Would they ever reach an understanding? Could they ever become friends? That was the story that twenty years later began finally to take shape in my mind."[2] Speare came upon the incident when she was in Maine on a fishing trip with her husband. Bored by fishing, she decided to explore the Milo library and discovered the anecdote.

Because of other work that she was doing, she did not begin to think about the possibilities of creating another novel based on this anecdote until much later. The resulting novel gives a reader who knows about the original incident a look at how Speare's imagination works. Basically, she incorporates the main incident but makes major changes throughout, leaving the reader with much more than a mere survival story. The reader cannot help but absorb the many facets of the Native American culture described in the novel, and out of that experience must come a new respect for that culture and the people.

Importance of Setting

The setting is once more in America, but this time the protagonist is younger: Matt turns 13 during the course of the story (Daniel in *The Bronze Bow* is 18, Kit Tyler in *Witch* is 16 and Miriam in *Calico Captive* is 14). His name, age, and the date (now 1768 instead of 1802) have been changed from the original. The location is the Maine wilderness (as in the original) where Matt and his father have journeyed to carve out a home. The book opens with Matt facing the prospect of seven weeks alone in their new cabin while his father returns to Massachusetts for the rest of the family. In his father's absence he must cope with his environment and with the few people he meets. The Maine forest in particular comes remarkably alive under Speare's pen: "Miss Speare is successful in drawing in the wilderness as an actor in her drama" (*CLR,* 211). As both adversary and ally, the forest creates problems and offers solutions for the protagonist as he learns from it and matures during the course of the novel. The possibilities of disaster on many fronts (from animals, terrain, weather) loom large among the forest trees, where Matt must take charge during his father's absence, caring for cabin and crops until the family is reunited. The woods become a testing ground for Matt: his bravery in the face of the surrounding wilderness and his skill in coping with it earn him the respect of his family. This setting also creates an atmosphere that readers absorb along with the adventures of the plot, so that they quickly come to feel the vastness and initial loneliness of the place.

There are fewer characters in this novel to interact with each other than in any of Speare's previous books, but she has created more interplay with the environment to compensate. Matt is soon without most of his food because of his carelessness and a marauding bear, and his rifle is stolen. Matt's lack of knowledge about people, the forest, and how to act in it is the catalyst for bringing him together with the Indian Saknis and his grandson (changed from the chief's son in the original incident). Furthermore, Speare deftly and imaginatively creates a relationship between Matt and the Indian boy, Attean, that parallels in reverse the relationship between Crusoe and Friday in *Robinson Crusoe,* which Matt is using to teach the reluctant Attean to read. This sequence of events is not in the original anecdote. Matt, the would-be teacher, instead finds himself learning survival skills from Attean (how to spear fish, how to make snares, how to blaze a trail and read signs, etc.). In the process he absorbs a respect for the Indian boy's skill, culture, and people. For example, he learns about the variety of tribes and their territorial rights, designated by markings on trees, which are respected by other Indians. Matt discovers that Christian and native beliefs may coexist, even within one Indian family: Attean's sister has been baptized, yet Attean still follows tribal ritual by going into the forest to seek his manitou, the spiritual guide that will make him a man and a hunter. The earlier French and Indian War has shown seeds of hatred between Indians and whites; through his challenging environment and his friendship with Attean, Matt discovers values other than those of white European culture, and with that discovery comes understanding and respect.

Style: A Study in Contrast

Speare uses the device of contrast effectively early in the novel when a white man, Ben, appears at the cabin. Matt distrusts him despite his cheerfulness and his good storytelling about Indians, especially about the Penobscots who inhabit the area in the summer. Without an invitation, Ben settles in for the night. When Matt awakens the next morning, he finds that the rifle his father left him has disappeared along with Ben. The white man's thievery is soon contrasted with the lifesaving kindness of the Indians. When Matt becomes entangled in the weeds of a pond where he had fled to escape a swarm of furious bees, an old Indian named Saknis rescues him. Saknis removes the stingers and carries Matt to the cabin.

When Matt has recovered, Saknis enters the cabin and asks him questions; Matt answers openly, for "it did not occur to him to lie to this old man as he had to Ben."[3] The differences between cultures and Matt's reactions to those differences soon begin to emerge. Matt, enrolled as reading teacher to the unwilling and resentful Attean, hears why Saknis wants his grandson to learn to read: "White man come more and more to Indian land. . . . White man make signs on paper, signs Indian not know. Indian put mark on paper to show him friend of white man. Then white man take land. Tell Indian cannot hunt on land. Attean learn to read white man's signs. Then Attean not give away hunting grounds" (*SB*, 31).

When Matt begins reading *Robinson Crusoe*, Attean is scornful of Crusoe's behavior. "White man not smart like Indian. . . . Indian not need thing from ship. Indian make all thing he need"

(*SB*, 38). Matt thinks of the scanty supplies he and his father had to work with in building the cabin and the furnishings, and he concludes that "Robinson Crusoe had lived like a king on that island!" (*SB*, 38). Interestingly, some writers in the eighteenth century felt the same way. J. H. Campe, in *Robinson Crusoe the Younger* (1779), has Crusoe cast away without tools or other aids. Later in the Defoe book, when Friday kneels down to Crusoe and offers to be his slave, Attean is furious: "Not be slave. Better die!" (*SB*, 43). Matt has never questioned that story before. "Like Robinson Crusoe, he had thought it natural and right that the wild man should be the white man's slave. Was there perhaps another possibility? The thought was new and troubling" (*SB*, 44).

From that point forward Speare has Matt see the Defoe book in a new light, through Attean's eyes, and he begins to make changes as he reads the book out loud to Attean, deleting the first words that Crusoe taught Friday ("master") and making the black man less thickheaded. "After all, there must have been a thing or two about that desert island that a native who had lived there all his life could have taught Robinson Crusoe" (*SB*, 46). At the same time, Attean teaches Matt survival techniques: how to set snares and how to catch fish with a sapling spear and hand-made lines and hooks. These hunting techniques are fully described in *Penobscot Man* (Speck, 48–49; 82–86), a book Speare used as part of her research.

Speare shows the growing trust and friendship between the two boys as Matt's education continues. "He remembered Robinson Crusoe and his man Friday. He and Attean had sure enough turned that story right round about. Whenever they went a few steps from the cabin, it was the brown savage who strode ahead, leading the way, knowing just what to do and doing it quickly and skillfully. And Matt, a puny sort of Robinson Crusoe, tagged along behind, grateful for the smallest sign that he could do anything right" (*SB*, 57–58). The role reversals are fully evident, but new contrasts continue to emerge. Attean shows Matt how to mark a trail secretly, not blatantly branding trees the way the white man does: "Indian maybe not want to show where he go" (*SB*, 57). Later, they find a white man's iron trap: "Indians not use iron trap. Iron trap bad" (*SB*, 63). Attean explains how the white man has corrupted some Indians to use the iron trap to hunt for pelts, and as a result there is no longer plenty of game available for food.

In addition to contrast, Speare makes limited use of foreshadowing, intriguing her readers and enticing them forward. While the book does not consist of cliff-hanger chapters as in a serial, chapter 2 ends with a hint of trouble ahead: "So he was not so quick-witted as he should have been when unexpectedly someone arrived" (*SB*, 10). The foreshadowing is not heavy-handed. Before the marauding bear ravages the supplies in the cabin when Matt forgets to secure the cabin door, Speare writes: "Perhaps he even became a mite careless" (*SB*, 19). His father's remembered warning about bees being "better left alone" (*SB*, 22) presages the dire consequences when Matt climbs the bee tree to get the honeycomb. Later, chapter 15 begins: "On the day of their greatest adventure, Attean had come without his dog. So there was no warning" (*SB*, 71). Such writing draws the reader through the story.

Portrayal of Native American Culture

In *The Sign of the Beaver*, Matt begins by thinking he has much to teach his Indian friend, Attean, but he soon discovers that Attean also has much to teach *him*. The novel can be seen as an introduction to and appreciation of Native American culture, in all its environmental specialization and harmony.

When *Robinson Crusoe* is finished, Matt turns to the Bible for stories. As he begins the story of Noah, Attean tells him that the Beaver people have a similar story, which sets Matt wondering again: "how could it be that here in the forest they had learned about the flood?" (*SB*, 70). Later, when the boys encounter a bear that Attean kills, the Indian boy startles Matt by asking forgiveness of the bear. After the bear meat has been taken to the Indian camp, there will be a feast, for "the Indians did not kill for sport" (*SB*, 75); the bear will provide much-welcome food. At the camp

Matt learns more of the Indian way of life: Attean will eat none of the feast because he was the successful hunter. According to Speck, "should he eat of it himself he would never get any more" (Speck, 47). Thus Attean proudly explains to Matt: "I kill. Not eat. Maybe not get any more bear" (*SB*, 82). The reader learns of the curiosity of the children, the work of the squaws, the laughter, shouting, and dancing at the feast, but also of the Indians' poverty. "'Indian not have money. One time plenty wampum. Now wampum no good to pay for gun.' . . . For the first time Matt glimpsed how it might be for them, watching their old hunting grounds taken over by white settlers and by white traders demanding more skins than the woods could provide" (*SB*, 87).

Matt's ignorance corresponds to the reader's; Speare gives both plenty to think about and to question. There is more to be learned, as Matt discovers that Attean's mother was killed by a white man: "My mother do them no harm. We no longer at war with white men. Just same they kill for get scalp. White men get money for scalp. Even scalp of children" (*SB*, 88). Attean's father went after the white men to seek revenge, but he never returned. When Matt tries to explain that white women are also afraid to leave their cabins, Attean's retort is, "Why white men make cabins on Indian hunting grounds?" (*SB*, 88). Yet that answer is negated later in the novel. For example, later Matt asks Attean if the land that the cabin is on used to belong to Attean's grandfather. "'I not understand. . . . How can man own land? Land same as air. Land for all people to live on. . . . Does deer own land?' . . . Somewhere in the back of his mind there was the sudden suspicion that Attean was making sense and he was not" (*SB*, 117). Yet why can't the white man build his cabin on the Indian hunting grounds without fear for his family since the land belongs to all?

When Attean and the other Indians break camp to move to hunting grounds unsettled by whites, Matt is offered a place in the tribe as Attean's brother. Matt refuses their offer with regret, for he has come to know and respect the Indians and to admire their freedom. Yet "he was bound to his own family, as Attean was bound to his grandfather" (*SB*, 114). Matt's having to choose "was not part of the original anecdote. But having introduced an English boy to an alternate way of life, and a very appealing way, it seemed to me important that he must make a choice" ("Survival," 168). Thanks to Attean and his lessons, Matt is now capable of surviving on his own and of making many items for his family (dishes, a birch broom, a cradle, a doll for Sarah, etc.); he can even do the work that was delegated to the squaws in the Indian camp. Such work keeps him busy and helps ease the loneliness, which is also ameliorated by Attean's departing gift of his dog. Matt's situation is comparable to that in Jean-Jacques Rousseau's *Emile,* in which the book's namesake learns from experiences in the outdoors rather than from books in a schoolroom. Matt, the supposed "teacher" who tries to use *Robinson Crusoe* as his text, instead learns survival techniques from his "pupil," Attean, while discovering that Crusoe and his white culture are not as superior as Matt had once thought. When his family eventually does return, in December rather than in August as planned, Matt's father expresses pride in his son for what he has accomplished, thus further affirming what Matt has learned from his Indian friends.

When asked about the Indian words in the novel that have no pronunciation guide, Speare explained that there was no such glossary in her book because "I don't know how to pronounce those words, but they are real words" (Interview). She continued, "My husband and I went up to Old Town in Maine and talked to a professor there, and he gave me some of the words that I needed. Also this Speck [Frank] who wrote *Penobscot Man* had a great many words listed that I could use, but no pronunciations. I found some others in Yale. I found a little book with Indian names in Yale which I also used in *Calico Captive*" (Interview). Again, there were no pronunciations. With regard to the Indian boy's name, "Attean," "I'm quite sure, although I've not read this anywhere, that it's probably a corruption of Étienne because they had so many French names—the priests would baptize many of the Indians and give them French names [Attean's sister Marie was baptized]" (Interview). Speare thus pronounces the boy's name as "Áh-tay-en." One note on the spelling "Attean": When Speare and her husband were in the Indian reservation of Old Town they came across several tombstones in a local cemetery with the spelling "Attean." Although the spelling in the historical incident was "Ateon," Speare decided to use what seemed to be the more common spelling, judging by the tombstone inscriptions.

Despite what Speare remembers, there *is* a pronunciation guide at the beginning of *Penobscot Man,* called "Phonetic Note" (Speck, vii); however, it may be more helpful to linguists than to the average reader, as the pronunciation of characters is explained in very technical terms: "*i*, high-front, unrounded; *e*, low-front, unrounded," etc. The name Attean appears with the Christian name associated with it, Étienne (Speck, 251). Since the priests were French Jesuits, the names are predominantly French. Interestingly, in *Penobscot Man,* the name Attean is found most often within the Squirrel family of the Penobscots and occasionally within the Sturgeon family, rather than within the Beaver band of Indians. Another Indian name used in *Calico Captive,* Sabbatis, also has a French Catholic equivalent mentioned earlier, Jean Baptiste (Speck, 249). Other Indian words that Speare uses—such as *ehe* (an affirmative), *nda* (a negative), *sigwan* ("spring"), and some others not translated in the novels— can be found in Speck's extensive study of the Penobscot Indians. The use of some Indian words adds a realistic flavor to *The Sign of the Beaver,* just as the French words and a few Indian words gave *Calico Captive* a distinctive touch. Children still write to Speare asking her if the Indian names are real (Telephone conversation).

A Question of Survival

Elizabeth Speare wrote *The Sign of the Beaver* with the relationship between the two boys, one white and one Indian, uppermost in her mind. "The relationship between those two boys was the main theme that I was interested in" (Interview). She was, therefore, quite surprised to learn from her Houghton Mifflin editor, Walter Lorraine, that she had written a survival story. After receiving her manuscript, he wrote: "On an audience level which I judge would be primarily middle-grade the adventure or survival theme would be the appeal. . . . in my opinion first attention should be to intensify Matt's surviving on his own."[4] Later Speare was to recall, "I was still naive enough when I reached the last page not to realize what had happened to my story, even though my publisher and the first reviewers recognized it at once" ("Survival," 163). Certainly the use of *Robinson Crusoe* helped encourage readers to recognize that the novel has survival as a theme, since the Defoe survival tale becomes central to the relationship between the two boys. Furthermore, when the Indians leave, Matt must use all of the knowledge gleaned from Attean to survive the wintry wait for his family.

The Lorraine letter demonstrates how an astute editor can encourage an author by recommending possibilities for changes that might make a manuscript more effective. Of course, it takes a talented writer to create fine material from the observations of an editor. It was Lorraine who observed that "Matt's new knowledge is never tested with the return of his father so close on the heels of Ateon's [the apparent spelling in the early version of the manuscript] departure. What did Matt learn from Ateon? Why does he immediately think of getting to town for goods? Perhaps here is an opportunity for Matt to test his adaptability and through some introspection nail down more firmly the worth of Ateon's Indian culture" (Lorraine). Such comments and others also reveal a little of what the original manuscript contained. Speare followed many of Lorraine's recommendations when she wrote the next draft of the manuscript. Originally, when the manuscript was submitted, "it was a good deal shorter than it is now" (Interview). Speare lengthened the end section and added material elsewhere in response to Lorraine's suggestions. For example, he wrote that "some scenes I feel could be fleshed out. I was disappointed that the first shot from father's gun is not described" (Lorraine). Speare not only added that episode but also showed how Matt discovered that he was going to have to practice with the beautiful gun to shoot effectively. Another comment was that "the scene with the bear [killed by Attean with Matt's help] seems a bit too fast. I would have liked a bit more foreshadowing and detail of Ateon's coming to manhood" (Lorraine). The foreshadowing that was added was mentioned earlier: chapter 15, about the encounter with the bear and her cub, begins with a reference to Matt and Attean's "greatest adventure" that happened without warning because Attean's dog was not with them (*SB,* 71). Speare followed both recommendations for adding material in the revision.

Lorraine saw that Speare's creation of "the relationship of Matt as a naive white and the wood-wise Indian Ateon is crucial" (Lorraine). He did think that some additions or further clarifications might be made in the boys' characterizations. He wrote, "Ateon is certainly superior to Matt in the woods but why wouldn't he pick up reading a bit more quickly and why wouldn't Matt try to learn some of his language?" (Lorraine). Speare obliged by having Attean be very reluctant at first but catch on speedily, "learning in spite of him [Matt]" (*SB,* 41) and despite Attean's own contempt for the language. Matt also begins to pick up and use some of the Indian words, and Attean also incorporates them in his conversations, knowing that Matt (and the reader by that time) can understand them.

There are some instances where the editor's suggestions were not followed. Lorraine wrote, "Robinson Crusoe is an interesting reference but perhaps too much is made of it" (Lorraine). Since there is a good deal of reading from the Defoe book in the final version, it is obvious that in this instance Speare felt that several selections were important for contrasting and comparing Attean and Matt with the Defoe characters and for revealing the Indian culture. When asked about that, Speare said that she felt it necessary to keep in the Crusoe references, and she did (Telephone conversation). She did not automatically accede to all of Lorraine's suggestions, especially if she felt strongly about what she had done; she always had the final say. Indeed, Lorraine himself wrote that "we will publish the book as you wish to write it" (Lorraine). One of Lorraine's further comments—"I would think you would have more drama if Matt innocently read the Friday reference without anticipation and then had to cope with Ateon's proud reaction" (Lorraine)—was certainly accepted. Matt's reading of the passage where Friday meets Crusoe and offers to be his slave elicits a violent response from Attean, revealing once more the Indian boy's fierce pride. Under those circumstances, Speare has Matt decide to do a bit of verbal editing of the sections he reads from then on. As an example, he wisely deletes Friday's calling Crusoe "Master" because he knows that Attean will be mightily offended.

In his letter to her, Lorraine commented on the episode with Ben, the white man who spends the night with Matt at the cabin and steals the gun. "The account of Ben is gripping and believable (although I rather expected to see Ben again later)" (Lorraine). Apparently some of her readers had the same reaction, for Speare heard from a few of them who felt the same way. Yet she had inserted Ben simply as a means of leaving Matt without the gun to help him survive, not as an added, recurring plot complication. Since she felt strongly that the story should not include a further meeting with Ben, that was how it was published. In each instance where editorial recommendations were made, the final decision to add, change, or leave intact was Speare's.

Endings and Beginnings

The Sign of the Beaver does not contain an afterword like the one in *Calico Captive* to explain the story's origin; that information is only available on the book jacket. Speare regrets the oversight. "I think it was just carelessness; it should have been in the book. I've got to have that changed" (Interview). In reference to selecting the tribe for her novel, she said that "there is a wonderful book called *Penobscot Man* and I used that. It has all the tribes listed. I chose the Beaver tribe because it's supposed to be extinct and I thought I would get into less trouble that way" (Interview). A chart of the tribes with their territories and origins in addition to other pertinent information can be found in Speck's book (213–15). The marking of family signs on trees to designate hunting grounds, described in *Beaver* by Attean (*SB*, 55–56), is also fully explained in *Penobscot Man* in a few places. For example, "the territory of each family group was regarded as inalienable property by the proprietors, to whom the hunting and fishing rights were restricted" (Speck, 206). Thus, when Attean and Matt find a fox caught in a metal trap, they do not touch it because the area is marked with the sign of the turtle.

Critical Reception

Speare's characters make a fine psychological study, for each boy has his own stereotypical view of the other at the beginning of the novel that gradually changes. The metamorphosis of each character is believable; their behaviors ring true. The final brotherly feelings of each boy toward the other have evolved naturally and realistically, not without some misunderstandings along the way. One reviewer comments, "Miss Speare's novel is a fine one, full of wisdom and practical good sense as well as understanding of human behavior under stress. It is an astonishing achievement for a writer."[5]

Although criticized by some because the conclusion is obvious from the beginning, as Jean Fritz observes in the *New York Times Book Review*—"it is no surprise that the family is long delayed and Matt is faced with unexpected difficulties"[6]—the book manages to rise above the predictable plot sequence through Speare's skillful characterizations and her evocation of a palpable wilderness. The focus therefore moves from a simple interest in the plot sequence to an interest in the growth of the friendship and understanding between the two boys. As cultures collide and traditional white values are questioned, young readers are forced to rethink their own attitudes and beliefs, usually ones that have been handed down to them through their families. This rethinking is similar to what older children or adults have to do when reading Conrad Richter's *The Light in the Forest*. In it a white boy, captured and raised by Indians as "True Son," with no memory of his white family, is forced to return to them by treaty. He expresses his attitudes and feelings in comments about the building of houses and fences, the restrictive clothing whites wear, and many of their other customs that have become ridiculous to him.

There is much more to both books than action and adventure, although both books have an ample supply of each.

Another criticism of *The Sign of the Beaver* has to do with Speare's use of stilted speech for Attean, called "stereotypical" by Barbara Elleman in her otherwise highly favorable review for *Booklist*.[7] Speare explains the use of typical speech truncations through the character of the white thief, Ben, who comments that the Indians know a little English picked up from traders (*SB,* 15), who most likely would have spoken to the Indians in just such a stilted fashion. Attean's use of English does improve somewhat with his increasing contact with Matt, and even though it remains choppy, it sounds much less abrupt later in the story than in the beginning. Apparently, children have no trouble believing in Speare's portrayal of Attean and the other Indians, for some have written to her asking, "Are you part Indian?" ("Survival," 169).

Although Speare says that Attean began to incorporate words like "verily" and "by golly," once they are mentioned those words never appear again. Such criticism is minor. On occasion, both Attean and Matt use Indian words. When asked why there is not more emphasis on caring for the corn, such a vitally important feature of daily life for the settlers (which she details in *Life in Colonial America*), Speare replied, "I never thought of that. . . . You do what you think of, that's all" (Interview). She does mention toward the end, when the Indians have left and Matt has chosen to stay, that "the corn he regarded as a sort of trust. His father had planted it and would be counting on it to feed the family through the winter. And some must be saved for the spring planting" (*SB,* 121). What Speare thought to include was obviously sufficient, for the resulting work merited high praise, including the prestigious Newbery Honor Book Award and the first Scott O'Dell Award for Historical Fiction. Speare has said that "each [survival] story is not merely a tribute to the ability of man or woman to endure and to meet extraordinary demands, but a record of spiritual growth, of the entering of the mind and heart into a new dimension and of a new appreciation of the wonder of life. All survivors bring with them on their return a new strength and certainty. They have learned that people can find in themselves the courage to go on—not to surrender to despair" ("Survival," 172).

These comments apply to the main characters in all of Speare's novels, not just to those in *The Sign of the Beaver,* as has been demonstrated through the discussions in the previous chapters. Speare has said that "young people need reassurance. They need to have confirmed their own sense of the rightness of things, of the value of loyalty, and especially of the bond of family" (*HB* 1989, 464). Each protagonist in her novels has shown a moral toughness and a resilience that enable him or her to withstand misfortunes. In each book there is a strong love of family. Yet the reader does not get a feeling of sameness from one book to the other, for the characters' similarities are subordinated to their highly particularized situations and personalities. It is to Speare's credit that she is able to succeed in creating such unique characters. Moreover, her novels for young people have been translated into several languages, including Japanese, German, Portuguese, and Afrikaans. Speare was especially taken with the Japanese editions because of the reading from right to left and because many little drawings were included (Telephone conversation). The translations show the universal qualities of the themes expressed in her novels and the strength of the characters that can reach out to children in a variety of cultures.

7

The New Freedom: *Child Life in New England, 1790–1840*

This little book, graced with numerous illustrations of toys and samplers and reproductions from early primers and other books, was one of a series of 20 volumes offered for sale at Old Sturbridge Village. Some others in the list included *Medicine in New England, The Village Mill in Early New England, A Primer of New England Crewel Embroidery,* and *Herbs and Herb Cookery through the Years.* As can be seen from the samples given, a wide range of topics was covered. The intended audience was obviously more adult than youthful, although Speare's prose in her contribution is accessible to young readers. Apparently, when Speare had agreed to write the book, one of the series was sent to her to use as a reference for general length, format, and style. She does not recall which booklet it was or if a contract had already been signed at that point. As far as she can recall, there was no pressure put upon her to finish it by a certain date. Speare's Old Sturbridge Village contribution, *Child Life in New England, 1790–1840,* was the forerunner of a much longer book, wider in scope and set earlier, that would be published two years later by Random House: *Life in Colonial America.*

The New Freedom

For children and adults who may have thought that childhood during the 50 years indicated in the title was a continuum of Puritan harshness, the first paragraph dispels that notion: "A visitor from France caught the spirit of new freedom and buoyancy which characterized the children of a new-formed and confident republic."[1] The American Revolution wrought many changes, not the least of which was a new attitude toward children and their upbringing. "At the turn of the century men looked to the future with confidence, and they looked at their own children, who would move into that future, with fresh appreciation and respect" (*CLNE*, 4). No longer relegated to the sidelines, children assumed their rightful place in the family. They still had household duties and moral obligations, but they now also possessed a freedom to behave as children rather than as miniature adults.

A good part of this new freedom originated in the influential theories of John Locke, who "had recognized that children were rational creatures, that they should be treated with consideration and allowed to be children" (*CLNE*, 5). Alice Morse Earle, in her *Child Life in Colonial Days*, one of the sources used by Speare, states that Locke's *Thoughts on Education* "is in many old-time library lists in New England, and among the scant volumes of those who had but a single book-shelf or book-box. I have seen abstracts and transpositions of his precepts on the pages of almanacs, the most universally circulated and studied of all eighteenth-century books save the Bible."[2] Locke's theories, widely adopted by parents, created a new world of childhood for many children.

Jean-Jacques Rousseau's even more liberal theories espoused in his book *Émile* had their influence, too, although the theories of both men regarding the treatment of children were more often implemented at home than in the schools. Speare points out that this new freedom for children had surprising results, for instead of creating a breed of spoiled, undisciplined youth, the opposite occurred: "The children, who were quick to seize upon their new freedom, soon proved its merits by a competence and productiveness that astonishes us" (*CLNE,* 5). It also freed the parents who no longer had to be constantly disciplining their offspring but who could enjoy them instead.

More Changes

Many changes grew out of the new freedom. Soon after the American Revolution, clothing was made to accommodate young bodies and their more exuberant movements—not to imitate the clothing of adults, as had been the case: "As soon as a boy put on breeches he dressed precisely like his father—in miniature" (Earle, 62). Books and magazines began to appear in quantity explaining how to raise this new group of children, for they were still expected to mind their manners and to apply themselves to the various tasks that needed to be done. "In this new teaching, the rod, though not altogether banished, was displaced by new persuaders, praise and pleasure" (*CLNE,* 7).

A description of what needed to be done followed. Girls' tasks (sewing samplers, cooking, spinning, quilting, embroidery, etc., and the running of a household), boys' tasks (providing firewood, tending animals, hauling water, gardening, etc.), and those tasks that they had in common, such as hemming towels and knitting mittens and suspenders (*CLNE,* 9), are engagingly described. Speare recounts that many chores had to be completed before the child went to school, and the rest afterward.

Education and Work

The schoolroom was the exception to the new freedom. "With few exceptions, schoolmasters were autocratic, harsh, and frequently brutal disciplinarians" (*CLNE,* 10). Imagination and entertainment were almost totally absent, except that children had to provide their own copybooks, pens, and other needed supplies and could be a little creative when doing so. Speare does not mention but Earle notes that "lead pencils were not in common use even

in city schools till this [the nineteenth] century. . . . Many a country boy grew to manhood without ever seeing a lead pencil"
(Earle, 78–79). According to Speare, often "the only Speller or
Arithmetic was the one volume that remained in the schoolmaster's hand" (*CLNE,* 10). Yet the children learned to write "delicate
and perfect inscriptions" (*CLNE,* 10) in that environment; they
also were allowed to show their talents on Last Day, when each
student who had survived in school spoke a piece before admiring
parents and friends. Speare noted from her reading of Edward
Everett Hale's *A New England Boyhood* that in some schools
there was a tradition of speaking pieces as often as once a month.
Hale wrote that "I owe to the public school . . . that ease before an
audience which I share with most New Englanders."[3] At the Boston Latin School that he attended for five years from age nine,
"the system of the school was rigid" (Hale, 36). The environment,
however, was not as harsh there as in other schoolrooms, as
Speare has noted.

A few boys went on to college, but "the majority of the boys and
all the girls left their school days behind them at the age of four-
teen or fifteen" (*CLNE,* 12). The rise of cotton mills and other
kinds of factories wrought further changes in the lives of women
and children, for the promise of employment and independence
lured many away from home and school. "By 1831 sixty-eight per
cent of the mill employees in the cotton industry were young
women aged ten and upwards, mainly daughters of New England
farmers" (*CLNE,* 12). Because many of the factory tasks were
simple and repetitive enough for children, "often entire families
went to work together" (*CLNE,* 13) to help earn money, or "the
daughter . . . went to work so that her brother might continue
school, and she considered it a matter of pride that by her help
he could go to Harvard or Yale" (*CLNE,* 13). Frequently, children
were forced to go to work to help support their families even
though they may have wanted to continue with their schooling.
Such was the case with Lucy Larcom, author of *A New England
Girlhood,*[4] a book Speare used as part of her research. Most children earned 20 to 25 cents a day for their labor. "'I go to work
before daylight,' a little girl of eight or nine years was quoted as

saying . . . 'and never leave it until it is dark, and don't make enough to support mother and baby'" (*CLNE*, 14).

Play and Stories

Other, more fortunate children, free of the mills, had plenty of opportunity for "unsupervised, unrestricted" (*CLNE*, 14) play. Boys especially had all of the freedom that the outdoors provided, to run, hunt, fish, swim, skate, play with hoops and kites, and ride horseback. The jackknife was also an indispensable accoutrement, often used for making useful items and toys. The game of marbles was popular throughout the period Speare covers and beyond (Earle, 375–76). Speare tells about Edward Everett Hale's privileged upbringing; raised in Boston, he found "home to be the happiest place of all" (Hale, 62), for there "we had almost everything we wanted for purposes of manufacture or invention" (Hale, 62). That comment did not mean that all of his time was spent indoors, for "there cannot be a square yard of the Common on which I have not stood or stepped, and the same could be said of most boys of that time" (Hale, 89). Hale also revealed that he learned to swim at a swimming school (Hale, 55–58), unlike boys in the country. These and other tidbits not included in *Child Life* are available in libraries for the inquisitive reader to discover, prompted by the curiosity Speare arouses by her varied interesting selections from secondary sources.

Girls had their dolls and doll furnishings and also were allowed to explore outdoors, although usually in a more demure fashion than their male counterparts. Girls apparently found the twice-yearly process of making clothes a fascinating experience, full of skilled activity: weavers working their looms, yarn being dyed, and scissors cutting into cloth. The clothes-making also included new boots, and when warm weather approached, the girls helped their mothers create new sunbonnets (*CLNE*, 21).

All children eagerly awaited the holidays: Election Day, Fourth of July, Muster Day "with much shooting and gingerbread" (*CLNE*, 21), and Thanksgiving. Christmas was not celebrated.

There were also parties in city and country, and the popular quilting bees. Boys' games included cricket and football.

Although *The New England Primer* continued its influence and was read by children throughout the period, Speare conjectured that "surely there were times by the winter fireside when even staid Puritan fathers unbent to tell their children tales remembered from their own childhood in England—Aesop's Fables, or the stories of Jack the Giant Killer and Tom Thumb" (*CLNE*, 23). Lucy Larcom remembers her sister telling the familiar tales— "Red Riding-Hood, the Giant-Killer, Cinderella, Aladdin, the 'Sleeping Beauty,' and the rest"—and also relating "most of the folk stories of Ireland and Scotland, and also the wild legends of Germany" (Larcom, 83). *Robinson Crusoe,* which became available in America in 1775, became immediately popular with children, a popularity that was to last for generations. Washington Irving's *Sketch Book* and the novels of Sir Walter Scott were also widely read by children. Larcom relates: "I read the 'Scottish Chiefs'—my first novel—when I was about five years old. So absorbed was I . . . that I crept into a corner . . . and read on through sunset into moonlight, with eyes blurred with tears" (Larcom, 105). Nevertheless, Speare points out that these were rare treats; most of the reading intended for children was dry stuff indeed, primarily designed "to instruct and edify" (*CLNE*, 24). One bright light was *The Boy's Own Book,* filled with instructions for making "water wheels, kites, electrical experiments, even fireworks and one's own lantern slides" (*CLNE*, 26), the sort of contents that would still appeal to boys today. Earle also points out that Isaiah Thomas was reprinting *Mother Goose's Melodies* about 1785 and other publications from John Newbery in England such as *Goody Two Shoes,* which were available to the fortunate children of New England who were given or loaned copies (Earle, 269–90).

Final Portrait

Speare concludes her little book with a few more examples of what children were and were not permitted to do from individual reminiscences, and if some of these memories seem idyllic, Speare points out that children "were not spoiled. They were taught by the example of their parents to stifle passion, endure physical pain, and, in times of stress such as thunderstorms, to remain calm" (*CLNE,* 27). Yet the overall picture remains of a happier, more carefree time than their peers enjoyed 50 years earlier, especially in New England.

As in all of her works, both fiction and nonfiction, Speare tries to give a balanced portrait of the period she covers, even in such a short booklet. Many curious facts had to be omitted, such as examples of precocious children discussed in *Child Life in Colonial Days*. Parents of these children tried to instill learning in their offspring when they were still toddlers: "Injudicious parents sometimes taught infants but three years old to read Latin words as soon as they could English ones" (Earle, 184). An even more startling example "is told of Timothy Dwight, President of Yale College, that he learned the alphabet at a single lesson, and could read the Bible before he was four years old. . . . he studied through a Latin grammar book twice without a teacher. . . . He would have been prepared for college when but eight years old, had not the grammar school luckily discontinued and left him without a teacher" (Earle, 184–85). The foregoing is just a small sampling of interesting omitted items; however, considering her space limitations, Speare chose wisely.

All was not sweetness and light in New England in the early nineteenth century; however, Speare does not dwell inordinately on the darker side of the period. Certainly if space had permitted, many more examples could have been given of the terrible drudgery in mills and factories, of the long hours that she alludes to, of the shortened lives caused by the stressful environment, the pollution, and factory accidents. Freedom, too, involved risk of serious or fatal accidents—crashing in a sled, falling off a horse, or drowning—as it does today. Speare's work serves to dispel the common notion that all children then led dreary, hard lives with little time to call their own. She has made the reader aware that there were close, loving families where children were treated as children and not as miniature adults. Although they had to learn to mind their manners, for good behavior was still important, those fortunate ones who did not have to spend all day in the mills enjoyed plenty of time for both learning and play.

Writing and Illustrations

Speare's writing in *Child Life* possesses the same ease and ability to hold readers' interest that later earned her much praise in *Life in Colonial America*. She draws from many first-person sources for arresting anecdotes that may easily prompt the reader to explore further in other books. From time to time she interjects questions (e.g., "What of the sisters of those very active boys?" [*CLNE*, 20]) to pique the reader's interest further, and she uses adjectives effectively, as in the phrases "spontaneous inclination," "unnatural demand," "exceptional situation," "gentle tolerance," "never-finished sawing," etc.

The illustrations chosen to accompany Speare's text, which appear at least on every other page, are a pleasing mixture of reproductions of paintings, reprints from period children's books and primers, and many photographs of period children's toys, including a tea set, skates, and snowshoes. The toys appear to be hand-carved, for the most part; the books are on a variety of subjects. The few reproductions of paintings are of the family or just of children, such as the cover portrait of a boy and girl, Joseph and Anna Raymond, from the National Gallery of Art. When Speare was writing an article for *Galaxy* magazine titled "School Days," about the colonial period, she went to a little museum in Wethersfield that had samplers, a schoolmaster's note to parents, and other period objects and reproductions. Some of those she used in *Child Life in New England*. Others came from the collection at Old Sturbridge Village (Telephone conversation). The resulting volume is visually pleasing, with the reproductions providing an interesting adjunct to Speare's engaging text.

This little book, only 27 pages long, seems to have escaped the notice of critics, most likely because of its limited distribution. It is a valuable document in the study of Speare's work because it reveals her selective talent, her ability to draw from a vast amount of research material the main points that a reader should know. At the same time, she shows her skill at presenting such information in an appealing style that keeps the reader turning the pages, curious to find out more. It is her stylistic ability to arouse and maintain interest that accounts for the success of her nonfiction.

8

The Heart of the Matter:
Life in Colonial America

In her single major nonfiction book, Elizabeth Speare shows the same enthusiasm for her subject that she exhibits in her novels. Although she delved into her research for this book in much the same way that she did for her fiction, the writing proved to be a different kind of challenge for her, primarily because of pressures from the publisher for her to submit work in progress.

Speare's research of the period was extensive, as evidenced by the breadth and depth of information contained in the volume. The focus is on seventeenth- and eighteenth-century life. "Old prints, the drawings of Charles Walker, and photographs of items now displayed in our historical museums illustrated her simple and direct prose" (*CLR*, 210). Yet she was

> just not happy doing it . . . That book was not written for Houghton Mifflin. It was an assignment more or less. I was contacted by Chanticleer Press and asked to do that, and I'll never do it again. It was contracted. Chanticleer kept calling me up and asking, "When is the next chapter coming?" and I don't like to work that way. Also, I didn't like the way that they worked with the illustrator that they gave me. . . . It worked out well enough, but I was not happy doing it. . . . I was independent by that time.

Maybe if I was a younger woman, I would have done more of those. (Interview)

Her reservations about the illustrations were confirmed by the reactions of at least one critic, Margaret S. Libby, who writes in *Book Week* that "Charles Walker's marginal and full-page pictures are the routine over-printed sketches we are used to seeing in texts and many Landmark books. . . . this good text deserves a Tunis as illustrator."[1] Alice Dalgliesh, in her comments for the *Saturday Review,*[2] also mentions the formula pattern of the illustrations.

Speare's research for this book, just as for her novels, was a labor of love. She is wise enough to "have a very strong feeling that you cannot crowd in everything. You can only use a fraction of what you have learned yourself" (Interview). Although she was talking about her historical novels, the same philosophy applies to the writing of an informational book about a period. Selectivity also prevents the reader from becoming bogged down by an over-whelming number of facts and perhaps giving up. She culled information from "diaries, letters, travelers' tales, and recon-structed colonial villages"[3] along with other sourcebooks on the period. From these varied documents she has created a viable, readable resource for young readers. Adults, too, can learn a great deal from the material presented.

Scope

The Virginia Experience
Speare begins her book with the founding of Jamestown, Virginia, and the hopes for gold that were soon dashed when the ill-pre-pared settlers were confronted with the hardships of their new environment. The various home constructions—beginning with wigwams or crude tents that became thatched one-room cabins and more pretentious dwellings as time passed and fortunes changed—are engagingly described, as are the furnishings of the different dwellings.

The reader learns about bonded convict labor and the growing slave trade as towns and plantations began to appear and houses and furnishings were upgraded. Speare describes in detail the lavish life-styles on the plantations and the number of slaves required to support them, including the estate of George Washington. The information contains enough detail to be fascinating without being overpowering, so that the reader does not become bored. Speare's description of the education of colonial children is especially interesting to the contemporary reader.

The New England Scene
The setting shifts to New England, from the Pilgrims at Plymouth (spelled Plimoth then) and the hardships, sickness, and failure of the ideal of common property (lots were later assigned) to Puritan settlements in Salem, Boston, and other New England towns and colonies. Readers were probably surprised to discover that early settlers lived in caves and wigwams and that later windows were sometimes covered with woodchuck skin. Another appealing tidbit is Speare's description of the tithing-man in church whose job was to tickle and/or rap snoozing parishioners. For this job he carried a stick with a knob on one end and a fox's tail on the other. Paul Fleischman describes his actions in his novel *Saturnalia,* set in 1681: "In fulfilling his duties at Sunday's church service, he'd banged the staff's knobs on the doltish heads of a variety of squirming, whispering, laughing, face-making, Satan-claimed children, while waking no less than four dozing adults with a tickle of the foxtail."[4] Boys were a special, more difficult problem in church, according to Alice Morse Earle. In *Child Life in Colonial Days* Earle mentions that the "tithing-man" had the help of two parishioners in trying to keep order among the boys, who became more and more unruly as the years passed: "By 1776 the boys were so turbulent, the spirit of independence was so rife and riotous, that six men had to be appointed to keep order, and they had authority to 'give proper discipline' if necessary" (Earle, 246). This account is not the usual picture that most people have of young churchgoers in the eighteenth century.

Speare contrasts the austerity of life in New England with that of a Williamsburg plantation with its many inns and coffee-houses, its luxury and beauty. The comparison is reminiscent of the differences Kit finds between her life on Barbados and what she encounters in Wethersfield in *The Witch of Blackbird Pond*. In the South there was much to entertain the general public as well as the wealthy: sports, races, dances, and shows of various kinds. The Sabbath was treated casually in Williamsburg compared to its importance and rigidity in New England. "For the Virginians, religion was never the heavy burden it was for the Puritans in the north" (*LCA*, 22).

New Amsterdam and Albany

Speare presents life-styles of farmers, fur traders, and the like as well as life in villages and in cities such as Boston. She moves from New England to life in New York (formerly New Amsterdam) and Albany. Speare explains that the first Dutch settlers came to make money from furs, "and their settlement was carefully planned from the start to reduce to a minimum the hardships of the New World" (*LCA*, 52). Dutch farmers built comfortable homes with several rooms and sturdy furnishings for the ample inhabitants, for the Dutch were fond of plentiful good food. Once education was introduced, it was provided for girls as well as for boys. Children in Albany also "had a freedom that no other colony allowed" (*LCA*, 60). Once a young man decided to marry, however, he had to go into the wilderness to prove himself for a year, then sell his furs to provision a ship for Bermuda "where he took on a cargo of rum, and sugar and molasses" (*LCA*, 60). Upon his return he could marry and settle down to farm or continue trading. Some Dutch did have slaves, but these were never sold to other masters (*LCA*, 62).

Backgrounds for Fiction

The section on Puritan New England contains some of the information that appears in *The Witch of Blackbird Pond*, such as the Sabbath houses for cooking, the Puritan disapproval of silk and bright colors, and Puritan beliefs about witchcraft (e.g., that witches are either old or young and pretty, that bewitched cows are immovable [i.e., the owners cannot get them to obey], etc). The section also relates that in Salem in 1693, 19 "witches" were put to death. Much of the entertainment found in *Witch* is also here, such as the cornhuskings, and a description of household furnishings that match those described in the book. In *Life in Colonial America* Speare mentions that "it frequently took a ship two weeks to make the five-day voyage up the Connecticut River from Saybrook to Hartford" (*LCA,* 135), information that she also uses in *Witch.*

Elements of the novels continue to appear. There is the isolated cabin in the woods; the importance of corn, mentioned in *The Sign of the Beaver;* the need for patience. Dr. Gershom Bulkeley—the famous physician who tends to the very ill Mercy in *Witch* and who is at odds with Matthew Wood over the king and the charter—is mentioned, along with his cures and medicine manual. Other sections describe the endless chores to be done, both inside and out: the weaving, candle making, embroidery, gardening, and the like, in addition to hunting and fishing for food. This book reveals that country boys as well as girls learned how to sew and knit. A boy's prize possession was his jackknife with which he whittled, carved, and made all kinds of implements for both hunting and playing. These chores also turn up in the novels, especially in *Witch* and *Beaver.* In the latter novel Matt makes a variety of kitchen implements for his mother with his knife: dishes, trenchers, bowls, even a cradle for the new baby. Later, in *The Prospering,* along with other details from her research, Speare will incorporate the colonial custom of drinking tea from saucers rather than from the cup in which the tea is served.

Speare describes the three most common dangers—wolves, Indians, and fire. She explains how hunting the numerous wolves for bounty became a popular sport. She also notes that there were often good relationships between Indians and whites, "but conflict was inevitable" (*LCA,* 84). She maintains her objectivity, pointing out the attacks on both sides. To combat fire, as Speare relates, laws were introduced everywhere, mandating that structures should have both ladders and buckets on hand. Some communities had fire wardens and some people whose homes caught fire were fined, but still the fires persisted. Boston's first fire engine came from England in 1659 (*LCA*, 94), and fire brigades became more numerous to cope with the menace. When a town had more than one brigade, "a fierce rivalry sprang up" (*LCA*, 94). Of these three dangers, real or perceived danger from Indians occurs most frequently and figures most prominently in her colonial novels.

Education, Trade, Crafts, and Transportation

In writing about the early schooling and children's primers, Speare describes the heavy moral emphasis and the morbidity of works such as *The New England Primer* with its alphabet in verse including the following: "While Youth do cheer / Death may be near" (*LCA*, 98). She writes: "Three-year-olds were required to memorize the Young Child's Catechism, which contained such warnings as: *Question:* What must become of you if you are wicked? / *Answer:* I shall be sent down to everlasting Fire and Hell among wicked and miserable creatures" (*LCA*, 98). Children in those early books often died young whether they were good or naughty, but the bad children always got their comeuppance.

Eventually real schools were established, but only for boys. "Ambitious parents taught their children to read when they were two or three years old" (*LCA*, 105). Both boys and girls could attend a dame school, a kind of kindergarten where children could learn their letters in addition to manners, some rudimentary math, sewing, and knitting. Eight hours daily in grammar school was the next step for boys, followed by college with even longer hours: "from six in the morning until dinner time, with enforced study in the evening" (*LCA*, 109). Not until the late eighteenth century were girls permitted to go to school, and then just for a couple of hours each day. "It was long after 1800 before girls attended the schools on equal terms with their brothers" (*LCA*, 113). There were no slates in the schools until 1820, and no blackboards or pictures. The children were supposed to acquire patience and self-control along with their learning of reading and writing (*LCA*, 112).

Speare devotes a chapter to "Tradesmen and Craftsmen" as she describes crops and trade. Fishing, whaling, furniture making, clock making, glassblowing, and the increasing importance of newspapers are delineated, along with England's attempts to keep the upper hand with the colonies through special laws and regulations. Cotton mills and their effects on children as well as on the general public are revealed, along with other information about the quality of items crafted at that time (e.g., beaver hats were made to last a lifetime or longer, for they were often handed down) (*LCA*, 133).

A chapter on transportation follows, describing all of the inconveniences, difficulties, and dangers involved in traveling by water, by foot (also called "shank's mare" [*LCA*, 134]), on horseback, or in various kinds of wagons and coaches. In boats there was the danger of overturning or of having to get out and help push or pull a recalcitrant craft. Footpaths presented other hazards such as fallen trees, marauding Indians, and rivers and bogs to cross, often in heavy clothing that would not dry well. Horseback was for those who could afford it; country people used oxen and springless carts for transportation. Coaches were reserved for the towns. With the growth of transportation came the post riders and circuit riders and the establishment of more inns and taverns, poor in quality at first but gradually emerging as clean and warm, with plenty of good food and genial hosts.

The book ends with a chapter on "High Days and Holidays," which begins by reminding the reader that throughout all of this activity and movement from place to place, hunting and fishing were still mainstays in the colonies, even if they were not indulged in as much by town boys. For other entertainment as well as necessity there were quilting bees, cornhuskings, bowling, cards, and dancing. The major holiday was Thanksgiving, although Speare notes that it was accorded its high status only gradually (*LCA*,159); Christmas was not celebrated at all until much later. As Speare explains, "Christmas had become such a rowdy and sacreligious holiday in England that the Puritans were determined to ignore it altogether" (*LCA*, 160).

Other holidays and entertainment included Guy Fawkes Day, Election Day, Independence Day, fairs, musical events, and horse racing. Theaters were thought of as evil and were frowned upon; still, they gradually began to appear, though not in the abundance of similar diversions. One recreation not mentioned as such in *Life in Colonial America* was explained in Louis B. Wright's *The Cultural Life of the American Colonies:* "In the modern world, we forget the sheer entertainment value of the church. . . . the sermon on Sunday and the sermon on 'Lecture Day'—usually Thursday—provided an interest that we find hard to imagine. The eloquence of some of the preachers was moving, and many of the congregation felt some of the catharsis of pity and fear provided by an Aristotelian tragedy. . . . In some communities the interest in sermons resulted in an excessive attendance at 'lectures' in addition to the regular church service on Sunday" (Wright, 187–88). The contemporary child may find that type of entertainment difficult to imagine.

Indexing: The Major Flaw
Unfortunately, the book's index is far too general to be of much use. Paul Revere is not even listed, for example, nor are Concord and Lexington. In terms of more general subjects, there are no entries for militia, schooners, primers, or dame schools. There is also no list of suggested further readings to encourage a curious child; the publishers "never made such a suggestion" (Interview) nor did Speare think of it. Nevertheless, as limited as this index might be, the Edwin Tunis book, *Colonial Living*,[5] to which the Speare book is usually compared, contains neither a suggested reading list nor even a general index (although it does contain a much more descriptive table of contents).

Style and Criticism

A Speare book is conversational rather than formal in tone, pleasing for both children and adults. Her text is called "fresh and interesting" by Margaret Sherwood Libby in her review for the *Sunday Herald Tribune*.[6] Other critics have noted that Speare "presents the material with unusual enthusiasm."[7] The *Christian Science Monitor* reviewer observes that "the use of words, the skillful presentation of facts so that they glow with interest will come as no surprise" to those who recognize that she "also wrote those two absorbing Newbery Award winning stories."[8] The *Saturday Review* critic writes that she "does not fail to make this account interesting to young people, though she never writes down to them" (Dalgliesh, 50), the last point being especially important when judging books for children.

Along with praise have come the inevitable comparisons to the Tunis volume. Esther Swift, writing for *Library Journal,* feels that the Speare book "makes a good companion to the Tunis volume."[9] She comments that *Life in Colonial America* is more panoramic in scope, rather than being "about the implements and appurtenances of everyday living" (Swift, 4489); however, the synopsis of the book given earlier indicates that Speare devotes considerable space to such "implements and appurtenances" and that they add to the book's interest. Zena Sutherland faults the organization: "The writing style is good, but the material is not as well organized as that of Tunis."[10] Certainly the Tunis table of contents offers the reader more specifics on each chapter than do the nine bare headings in *Life in Colonial America.* Within the Speare chapters, however, there are highlighted subject divisions, as in the Tunis volume, which provide an adequate amount of information and organization.

Although both books have a certain amount of information in common, each includes many different selections from the numerous research possibilities. Tunis, for example, mentions that the first Jamestown settlers were greeted by a shower of arrows (Tunis, 19); he further explains about the Indians and their behavior. Speare concentrates instead on the trials facing the new homesteaders, such as the shortage of iron nails: "If a man moved or built a new house he burned down his old one just to salvage the nails" (*LCA,* 7). She also pays more attention to the furnishings of that early settlement than Tunis does.

The same kind of comparisons can be made throughout the books. It is true that Speare's *Life in Colonial America* tends to skip from place to place more than *Colonial Living*. It is also true that because of the detailed contents a particular subject might be easier to find in Tunis's book, even taking into account the index in Speare's book (ferries, for instance, are part of the table of contents in Tunis, but there is no entry for them in Speare, although she does write about them). Both writers comment on the durability of beaver hats, but where Speare devotes only a paragraph to the subject, Tunis chooses to elaborate more fully on the difficult process of making them, including the procuring of pelts from New Netherland and New France (Tunis, 65–66). There is no entry for beaver, pelts, or hats in the Speare index, but there are four entries for "furs." Under one of those is the section on beaver hats. The reader must thus work a little harder to locate specific information in the Speare book.

Criticisms about the illustrations in *Life in Colonial America* were previously mentioned. Certainly the mixture of drawings with old photographs of an assortment of objects is pleasing. Some of the old prints are fascinating, such as the one that shows volunteers fighting a fire (*LCA*, 96), and there are also numerous interesting photographs of toys, tools, and household implements. Overall, there is a variety to the illustrations that is missing in the Tunis book. However, when the drawings in each volume are directly compared, those by Tunis appear to be far better, in particular sharper and more detailed. He is especially good at showing individuals working with implements, such as women working at a loom or spinning wheel and men using a flax brake, a swingling flax, or an adze on large timber. Tunis also often includes insets with enlarged details from his original drawing to help the reader understand even more fully. He does the same thing for the clothing worn so that some of the details of dress can be more easily seen. The Charles Walker drawings, on the other hand, usually have a colored wash over them that tends to obscure rather than clarify. Although Walker's illustrations look more like paintings than drawings and he frequently depicts action scenes that readers enjoy (see the Yale College students, *LCA* 111, and wrestling, *LCA* 91), the clarity of the Tunis drawings serves the informational purpose best.

Conclusion

Life in Colonial America has only minor flaws compared with its readable, engaging style that holds the reader through to the end. As part of that style, Speare occasionally injects rhetorical questions, which she then answers: "Why were so many rules and regulations needed if the Puritans were always stern and sober? Just a glimpse at the fines imposed in any town meeting shows us that the Puritans were certainly human. And we are misled by pictures which show them always dressed in black and gray" (*LCA*, 34–35). She continues in this instance to describe their dress. One piece of information in *Life in Colonial America* relates to the parishioners' reaction to Kit's appearance on her first Sabbath in Wethersfield in *The Witch of Blackbird Pond:* "Silk in any form was frowned upon, since it was both costly and perishable" (*LCA*, 35). Only if a woman was known to be wealthy could she wear silk. Thus Matthew Wood's negative reaction to Kit's silk finery is understandable. In another example from *Witch*, the wealthy Mistress Ashby wore damask (a cloth of silk or linen; probably silk in this instance) trimmed with lace, perfectly acceptable attire for her because of her known status.

Speare often chooses expressive verbs in her descriptions ("bridges spanned," "shelves displayed"), and on rare occasions she uses an exclamation point for added emphasis. When describing the threefold weaving process, she tells the reader: "To weave about three yards of cloth, a good day's work, the weaver had to repeat these three steps three thousand times!" (*LCA*, 80). Her sentences roll easily off the tongue and produce vivid images: "We who have never waked in the night to the cry of wolves cannot imagine the terror this sound brought to the early settlers. At night one could see the menacing eyes glowing on the outskirts of a campfire, and even in the daytime shadowy forms haunted the edges of fields. The cry of a pack . . . must have chilled a settler's blood" (*LCA*, 83). Such descriptive prose would hold any child's attention, and the writing continues to absorb the reader throughout. A reader already familiar with any of Speare's novels with a New England setting should find the information in *Life in Colonial America* intriguing when bits of it are remembered from her fiction. Not only does a child then get to absorb the material in the nonfiction work, but he or she gets to see how a writer incorporates research into fiction, fleshing out the story and making the time and settings come alive.

9

Generations: *The Prospering*

In *The Prospering* a real person once again becomes the impetus for Speare's fiction—in this case a novel for adults. Although Speare has said that she does not have a particular age group in mind when she writes her novels, she soon realized that her own interests in Jonathan Edwards and other religious material she uncovered obviously would not appeal to younger readers, and so she decided that this book would be for an older audience.

In her foreword Speare explains a little of the background of the book, including her adherence to historical fact: "To the recorded facts I have been, to the best of my knowledge, scrupulously faithful. The personalities of the men and women of Stockbridge, revealed by their own writings and by the judgments of their contemporaries, I have attempted to convey accurately."[1] During skiing trips with her husband, Speare consulted journals, public records, and genealogies at the Stockbridge library, the Williams College library, and the Williamstown library, attempting to find out as much as possible about the people who had actually lived who would inhabit her novel. For Elizabeth Williams, the heroine of *The Prospering*, as for Miriam Willard in Susanna Johnson's captivity narrative, the record was so scanty that Speare was once more at liberty to use her imagination freely: "Of the eighty-two years of her life there are only two witnesses—a chair cover embroidered in her youth and the conventional eulogy delivered at her funeral. . . . For the undocumented history of mind and heart I alone am answerable to Elizabeth Williams" (*P,* vi).

The novel began with outlining, as did most of Speare's other books except *The Witch of Blackbird Pond.* Here it was mandatory in order to keep the families straight. "*The Prospering* I did almost entirely by outlining because that was entirely historical . . . and I made columns of each of the people in the family—what they were doing every year. I had that right down through the years" (Interview). Because there were several families to keep track of, outlining was the logical way to proceed. The research took about three years for this adult book, double the time for her novels for young readers: "It took about one and one-half years for the young people's books" (Interview). Her research at the end began to blend in with the writing, for she was constantly going back and forth to the library to answer questions that cropped up (Interview). She wrote at the time, "Something comes up every few days—the research did not stop" (Letter 1).

When asked what differences there were between writing the four novels for young people and writing *The Prospering,* Speare responded: "No difference at all except that I was fascinated by the theology and the philosophy of Jonathan Edwards and that group of people in New England, and I knew that young people would not be interested, so it became a heavier book for that reason" (Interview). She added that she enjoyed writing *The Prospering.* Because of her love for the material, this book was the most difficult to stop researching and begin writing. Even then, "the research went on to the last chapter" (Letter 1). Anne Barrett, her editor, commented on it: "I cannot close without expressing my admiration for the amount of research you must have done and for your unobtrusive use of it. So often, in a book of this kind, stray bits of information (achieved, no doubt, after days or weeks of patient digging and therefore precious to the author) are included when they add very little to the story or the reader's understanding. I never felt this in *The Ice Glen.*"[2] During a telephone conversation in May 1990, Elizabeth Speare explained that *The Ice Glen* was her original title, which she still prefers. It was changed to *The Prospering* because those in charge of sales at Houghton Mifflin felt that it sounded too much like a juvenile title, and since they wanted the public to realize that this new novel was for adults, a departure from her previous works, they asked her to come up with something different. She chose four alternative titles, finally settling on *The Prospering*.

As with the *The Bronze Bow,* Speare suffered through a false start with *The Prospering*. "I had a vague notion of alternating sections of the book between Abigail and Elizabeth [they are sisters]. I sent the first two sections [to the editors] and they didn't like that. They felt it was too distracting, so I dropped Abigail and took it all through Elizabeth which was much better" (Interview). As Anne Barrett wrote her, "Our most basic criticism is of the device of dividing the narrative between Elizabeth in the first person and Abigail in the third. All our readers have felt that Elizabeth comes through much more clearly than Abigail. This may be in part because Abigail's story is told in the third person. It would be better if she told it herself, but we believe it might be still better if Elizabeth were the narrator throughout" (Barrett 1). Because there was no documentation on Elizabeth, Speare was fully able to create her own imagined character; she would have been far more restricted by the numerous available facts when working with Abigail.

Setting and Characterization

Although readers gain a strong sense of place in this book just as in Speare's historical novels for children, especially at the beginning when the Williams family is the first of the new settlers to arrive, setting gradually loses its dominance to the strong-willed characters who have come to tame it, to make a proper settlement out of its wildness. In this book, setting is subordinated to relationships, to the demands of characterization and the interest in philosophy and religion, thereby influencing the plot much less than in Speare's earlier books and contrasting sharply with her later novel, *The Sign of the Beaver,* in which setting is central to the action. In *The Prospering,* Speare concentrates on the characters' reactions to each other, from John Sergeant's amazement upon seeing Abigail for the first time; to Mrs. Williams's reaction to Mrs. Woodbridge, the schoolmaster's wife; to the Indians' response to the settlers, and vice versa. Distinct personalities quickly emerge as cultural differences and religious attitudes gain prominence over setting, affecting the actions of the principal characters throughout the novel as the town grows and prospers.

The decline in the prominence of setting does not mean that it is not distinctive; indeed, early in the novel the Ice Glen has a profound effect on Elizabeth, after her terrifying experience there when her foot is caught in the rocks and she is afraid that she will die. It is a place of evil for her from then on and is also the title of one of the five main sections of the book (not counting the prologue and epilogue). As the town grows, interior settings become more and more prominent as the characters meet and air their often contrasting views; exterior settings begin to lose their significance, except, perhaps, for the weather, illness, and discomfort they bring. Yet even the blizzard that traps Liza with the very ill David Brainerd and his Indian helper, John, becomes secondary to the ill man's ravings, her feelings, and her attempts with John to nurse David.

Later in the novel, after Liza has enrolled in a school in Boston, she attends a cousin's wedding in Wethersfield, Connecticut. It is now 1746, not the 1687 of *The Witch of Blackbird Pond,* and the town has changed remarkably. It is now "a pretty town . . . with a wide, tree-shaded green, flanked on either side by comfortable houses with green grass and flower gardens" (*P,* 273). Interior furnishings are even more impressive: "There were fine Chinese porcelain and English china. . . . We walked on soft woolen carpets . . . and the walls were covered with wallpaper from France. . . . There was a harpsichord in the parlor" (*P,* 273–74). These furnishings do not even belong to an extremely wealthy family, for there are no servants. It is quite a change from what Kit encountered during her stay in the same town.

Characterization is the strong point of the book, which uses first-person narration and flashbacks, two departures from Speare's earlier novels. "Adult human nature and motives are explored in much more depth than in *Witch,* for example, where the adults are often one-dimensional" (Interview). The book opens with a prologue set in Stockbridge in 1784 but quickly returns to 1737 and Elizabeth's arrival with her family when she was only seven. Except for the schoolmaster and his wife and infant, the Williams family is the first white family to come to the area. The next 23 years are chronicled principally in highlights, with a strong focus on characterization and relationships.

Elizabeth is the spunky one from the beginning, enjoying the adventure of the move, much to the delight of her father. Her reaction is quite the opposite of that of her mother and her siblings, who were all opposed to the move from the beginning. Her mother is in tears through most of the journey. Abigail, 16, is horrified and furious when she learns about their planned relocation, for she sees any chance for marriage disappearing in the wilderness. Josiah, also 16, runs away from home for two days before giving up and reluctantly joining in the emigration. Enoch, 2, Elijah, 4, and Judith, 8, comprise the rest of the children. Uncle Josiah is also a member of the party; his family is due to arrive later.

More of Elizabeth's (Liza's) character is revealed when the family stops at one tavern en route and Liza sees a dog turning the spit that holds roasting meat by walking on the steps of a wheel. With each step the wheel turns, which in turn moves the spit. Liza is horrified, for she knows what an uncomfortable chore it is when she has to stand by the hot fire even for a short time to turn the roasting meat. The thought that the dog will spend his entire life at that task is too much for her, and she brazenly asks her father to buy it. His own character takes on additional color when he at first refuses until he realizes what the dog does; then he brooks no nonsense from the reluctant landlord about buying the sad-looking animal. Liza's love for her father, always strong, grows even more steadfast from that time on: "Nothing that happened in all the years to come could ever crush out the love for my father that rooted itself that day in my child's heart" (*P*, 20).

Gradually other characters appear. The first is John Sergeant, a minister, already living on the site of the future settlement, who is there to greet them upon their arrival and who is immediately taken with Abigail; they will eventually marry. Mrs. Williams's tears stop flowing when she learns that Mrs. Timothy Woodbridge has a new baby who will need her help, and the future looks a little brighter for her. Of course, there are many problems and confrontations. John Sergeant is trying to do his best for the Indians, for example, and he is appalled when Liza's father gives them liquor to get them to work for him. To make matters worse, Mr. Williams shows no sign of contrition or repentance. He persists in using liquor as an incentive for getting prompt work out of the Indians whenever it suits him.

Liza's character emerges even more strongly when she pleads to be allowed to go to school with Elijah and the Indian children. When that privilege is denied her, she goes off with her reluctant younger brother and his equally disapproving Indian friends to see some caves in the woods. Once there the siblings are deserted and become lost, and Liza's foot gets caught in rocks. Fearing death, she reflects on her wickedness, but they are saved the next morning by the Indian Konkapot who carries her to his wigwam and sets her broken bone. When her father arrives, he is angry because of the fright the children have given everyone, especially their mother. As previously mentioned, after this incident the glen becomes a place of evil for Liza, especially at night. In spite of her spunky nature, she is not without fear.

Liza is given freedom to go to the Indian camp, where she becomes good friends with the Indian girl, Catharine, and learns much about Indian customs and their way of life. Soon she becomes envious of the casualness of their lives, especially their eating whenever they are hungry rather than at set mealtimes as she is required to do. She gives Catharine her gold locket in gratitude for all of the things Catharine brought her while her leg was mending, but when her mother finds out about the gift, she is horrified, and Liza's father tells her that she must go to Catharine and get the locket back. Although Liza fortuitously gets some beautiful beads to help with the exchange, Catharine apparently understands more than she lets on. Barrett wrote to Speare about the relationship: "Elizabeth's friendship with Catharine, the substitution of the blue beads for the locket, the reluctant drifting apart—all this is touching and revealing" (Barrett 1). Liza's friendliness with the Indians is not shared by her sister Abigail who, even after her marriage to John Sergeant, refuses to let the Indians come into her house to go to see him in his study. She demands that a separate back passage be built for that purpose. Although she is happy with John, she never loses her repugnance for his flock. Even when her half-brother, Ephraim (Eph), asks her to have King Hendrick, an important Indian, to tea, she refuses. When she later offers to teach a sewing class for Indian girls, though she lacks the patience needed for such a task, it is not because her thinking about Indians has changed. She takes on the sewing class for pragmatic reasons.

The novel then jumps ahead five years (almost two-thirds of the book takes place up through Liza's twelfth year) to when Liza is 17, and new people arrive. Liza matures; she learns from her mother how to care for the sick, and she falls in love with David Brainerd, a new minister who has come to preach Jonathan Edwards's belief in the elect, to her horror. While she yearns for David despite herself, Sam, one of the young men from the town, comes courting. Their courtship lasts four years and finally makes her acceptable in the eyes of the other girls her age, who eventually welcome her into their society.

Yet Liza seems to be thwarted constantly. After waiting years for David (while she keeps Sam dangling), she learns that he has died at the home of his fiancée (she had not known of his engagement), one of the daughters of Jonathan Edwards. Later, finally married and eager to have children, she discovers after a miscarriage that she will be unable to bear any more. Ironically, her sister Judith, who had abhorred the physical side of marriage and had never wanted children, marries a minister, goes through a healthy pregnancy and an easy birth, and becomes a doting mother. The last blow occurs after Liza's marriage to Stephen West, a new and moderate minister who believes that God's grace may be attained through good deeds. Subsequently he becomes filled with self-doubt, undergoes a conversion to a belief in pre-destination, the theory of Jonathan Edwards, and becomes un-compromising in his preaching. Although he is highly respected, his reputation reaching beyond the town, his views are not shared by Elizabeth. She has had a great deal with which to contend.

Speare maintains that "Abigail is the hero, the dominant one" (Interview). She is not afraid to voice and to fight for her opinions, even when they differ from those she loves. She never overcomes her dislike for the Indians despite all of John's talk, and she has some of her father in her as she caters to her personal vanity by spending Indian-fund money on clothes without a qualm. Her father also uses the Indians whenever it suits him without hesitation. Like him, she has a desire for power as well as wealth. She maintains her beauty and charm as the years pass, remarrying after John's death although her choice shocks Liza.

John Sergeant, from his first appearance when he is instantly smitten with Abigail, is a warm, fully fleshed-out character. He eventually becomes a loving husband, yet he is often distracted because of his feelings of responsibility for his Indian flock and his own mixed feelings about his abilities, accomplishments, and religious beliefs. Speare drew on his own account in developing his character: "John Sergeant's self-doubts were in his journal—he kept a wonderful journal" (Interview). Speare does an excellent job of capturing some of those self-doubts in her novel. She also believes that the real John was far-seeing about the Indians, although perhaps with limitations: "I think that John loved the Indians though I don't know that he understood them" (Interview).

Ephraim Williams, Liza's father, begins as a one-sided, dominant, willful character who does exactly what suits him regardless of what anyone else thinks. His drive is for wealth and power, and if he must bend rules to achieve his ends, so be it. Abigail has inherited that character trait. His conniving and high-handed tactics alienate members of the community. As the years pass, he gradually becomes more multidimensional. Physically, he becomes wracked with gout and suffers a serious illness from which he never fully recovers. In addition, he loses his power over and his grip on the community. Elizabeth, playing cribbage with him throughout his slow recovery, sees him with new eyes: "When I looked at the man across the table, I no longer saw either a god or a tyrant. I saw my father. . . . I loved him, if not just as I had loved him in childhood, at least as I had never been able to do in the years between" (*P,* 301). His one last attempt at regaining his position by buying up land fails, and he leaves Stockbridge, never to return.

Liza's mother also begins as a one-dimensional character, doing nothing but cry on the trip to Stockbridge, but she eventually develops a distinctive personality, especially when she begins to include Liza in more of her activities. Editor Anne Barrett was impressed with that relationship: "I also liked especially the parts about Elizabeth and her mother tending the sick" (Barrett 1). Mrs. Williams defers to her husband on most matters, such as in what should be done about the heirloom locket Liza has given to Catharine, but she can also show some independence. When she hears that members of the Edwards family are ill, she sends Liza to them with some calf's-foot jelly. Still, even then her sense of place in the family, of doing what is expected of her, is not fully overcome: she admonishes Liza not to say anything to her father since he wants them to have nothing to do with the Edwards family.

Some other characters, although numerous, are not as fully delineated. With the Jonathan Edwards family, for example, "much of that was fiction, but the characters were not" (Interview). The Edwards girls, known to Liza, are described most often as a group in terms of their characterization rather than as individuals, although Liza does find a friend in Sarah, the mother. It is hard to differentiate among the daughters at times. Four of them live at home; others come for visits. Even Mrs. Edwards is primarily known for her proud beauty most often displayed at the Sabbath meetings. She is the mainstay of the family; "there was about her something apart and untouched and serene" (*P*, 312) that Liza finds particularly comforting. The family patriarch is revealed through his sermons, conversations, and what others say about him. Although he remains at Stockbridge for 10 years, his characterization is not as developed as John Sergeant's.

An interesting sidelight is the death of little Enoch Williams, Elizabeth's brother. "I wanted to have a baby die. For some reason I just wanted that as part of Elizabeth's experience, and I finally had to use one of the other English families for the baby dying. . . . Then I found an entirely different genealogy. . . . Imagine it, there was a baby who died in childhood that had never been mentioned in any of the other genealogies. . . . It's funny how strangely things do drop into your hands" (Interview). Of course, if Speare had not been diligent and had not returned to the library for more research, she would not have encountered that new genealogy and would not have discovered her "lucky" find.

Style

Speare's style once more garnered applause. Sister M. Marguerite says, "Adhering rather closely to facts and to actual characters, Miss Speare clothes the dry bones of records with a vividness that causes the reader to relive the actual scenes."[3] Discussions at the dinner table reveal attitudes and facets of characters as well as religious beliefs and doctrine. Speare also uses the title ironically, for although the town prospers numerically, it is divided spiritually. Moreover, many of the main characters, although appearing successful to an outsider, do not fully succeed or, like John Sergeant, are filled with doubt about their achievements. Although Elizabeth has survived to see a high point of her husband's career and is a person many others may envy, she has faced numerous disappointments. Her father also has seen better days, becoming "a prisoner in his own castle" (*P*, 299) because of his gout and the enmity of many of the townspeople. There are even threats of tarring and feathering him (*P*, 304). When he leaves home abruptly to try to secure the backing of influential people elsewhere and that also fails, he exiles himself to Deerfield where he dies two years later.

The prologue is filled with the repetition of "prospering" so that the sense of future success is planted early, only to be put out of reach of the main characters as the novel progresses. Their lives are filled instead with ironic prosperity, for often appearances belie what is really occurring within the individuals. Some, like Ephraim Williams, find themselves devoid of the respect of the town when their past actions catch up with them. For example, just when Abigail and her new husband, Gen. Dwight, appear to be running the Indian school the way they want—for their own personal gain—they lose their hold on the school and their standing in the community. As Anne Barrett observed, "The book's theme is the failure of an experiment nobly conceived and executed by for the most part well-meaning but always fallible men."[4] Abigail is further distressed when her son John, by her first marriage to John Sergeant, decides to follow in his father's footsteps and become a minister to the Indians. The reader learns in the epilogue that when the Indians move farther west, John goes with them. The prologue and epilogue round out the novel, providing the circular framework for the plot.

As was the case in her earlier novels, Speare is objective in her portrayal of the Indians. Barrett recognized that in the manuscript. "One of the best things in the book is the description and interpretation of Indian-white relationships. I feel as if I not only knew more but understood the basic problems as I never had before" (Barrett 2). Speare shows the prejudice of some whites as the years unfold and the French and Indian War begins and ends. The soldiers especially, stationed in the town, "were contemptuous of our Indians. . . . They couldn't seem to get it through their heads that the Indians weren't our slaves" (*P,* 201). Speare later speaks through Liza's half-brother Ephraim when he says, "These missionaries come here to teach the Indians. Do they ever consider that the Indians might be able to teach them something too? . . . The Indians have a Great Spirit of their own, and moral laws that they hand down to their children. The Six Nations have an extraordinary system of government. . . . We must root it all out, simply because it's Indian" (*P*, 291). Eph even disparages John Sergeant because John had always referred to the Indians as his children. "Damn it, Liza, they're not children, and they're not creatures. Those miserable heathen redskins are men, and they want to be treated like men" (*P*, 292). Speare has praise for the Indians' payment to a family for the killing of a member: "Some would call it barbarous, this willingness to accept money in payment for a life; actually, it is an insistence on a man's worth, and at the same time a very sensible way of avoiding repeated bloodshed. It is a pity that the learned gentlemen of our courts have never bothered to understand an Indian's way of thinking" (*P*, 308). Earlier in the novel the reader learns how Indians have been cheated out of their land by unscrupulous whites giving them individual parcels, then running the Indians into debt and taking the land as payment.

In her previous novels Speare used some foreshadowing, and she uses it here as well, sparingly. For example, when David Brainerd, the new missionary, is talking about the Indians and salvation with John Sergeant, Liza feels that "there was a quality in the caring [David's] that made me uneasy even then" (*P*, 156). Later, Captain Kellogg agrees to take some Indian boys into his house "to teach them farming and some reading. . . . John made a tragic choice, but how can he be blamed that there was no one worthier of his trust?" (*P*, 203). Patience, a virtue extolled and repeated, especially in *The Witch of Blackbird Pond,* reappears to a much lesser degree here. Mr. Woodridge needs it to teach the Indians; and Liza, the tempestuous, sometimes outspoken child, gradually achieves it as she helps Abigail through her sick pregnancy. Later, when she can no longer keep silent about her love for David Brainerd and discloses to him her intention to leave with him, he tells her that she cannot go with him for a reason he cannot divulge, but she is able to wait for him for two more years until she learns of his death. She also discovers that he was engaged to marry one of Jonathan Edwards's daughters. Even then, she conceals her grief until Eph takes her to the Indian ceremony for the dead where she undergoes a healing catharsis.

One feature of this novel that makes its appeal more adult has already been mentioned: the weaving in of a great deal of theology as the various ministers come to the Williams home or as Liza hears their sermons in church and conversations elsewhere. Children's devotional books such as those Liza read as a child (e.g., *Pilgrim's Progress* and *A Token for Children*), are of less importance here than in *The Witch of Blackbird Pond,* where the hornbook Prudence uses is central to the story. Although there are revelations about theology in the latter book, which is meant primarily for young people, the religious discussions are far more detailed and profound in this adult novel. Religion is also more lightly discussed in *Calico Captive,* as Miriam Willard comes to see that Catholicism is not as bad as she has been led to believe. Yet among the more serious, complex theological discussions in *The Prospering,* there are lighter, questioning moments as well. For example, Liza's father buys a set of playing cards "surreptitiously, for there was a heavy fine on the sale of them" (*P,* 300). Seeing the pleasure they give, Liza expresses her views: "To tell the truth, to this day I do not understand what was so wicked about those cards" (*P,* 301).

Liza's religious upbringing is Calvinistic, and at first she accepts it without question. "Up to the time of David Brainerd's coming it had never occurred to me that a single word of Christian doctrine could be a matter of debate" (*P,* 146). Brainerd's doctrine is referred to as "New Light"—he is a follower of Jonathan Edwards—and his religious philosophy is one that Liza's father cannot abide. Liza learns from Abigail that "the New Lights believed that only a few were elected to be saved. All the rest were doomed, predestined to eternal punishment, no matter how they repented or pleaded" (*P,* 149). Liza is horrified. Later she sees how John Sergeant wrestles with his doubts about religion and eventually how her own husband, Stephen, will move from his rather liberal thinking to the rigid doctrine espoused by Jonathan Edwards, with its "test of conversion which none in Stockbridge attempted to meet" (*P,* 342). Liza sees the changes beginning in Stephen with growing concern: the feverish reading far into the night and the despondency as his doubts grow. He becomes more and more troubled, especially after long theological discussions with Mr. Hopkins, a firm believer in the elect. Hopkins tells Stephen: "A true Christian gives himself into the hands of God saying, 'May God be glorified, let what will become of me'" (*P*, 342). He further poses a question that tortures Stephen until his conversion: "Suppose he feels it most for his glory and his infinite benevolence that you should be damned?" (*P*, 343). As a result of these talks, further persuasion, and increasing self-doubts, Stephen succumbs to a belief in the elect.

These and many other theological discussions lift *The Prospering* out of the ranks of children's books, even though much of the novel takes place before Liza turns 13. The character of Liza, too, is the focus of the story from age 7 to age 54, a far wider time span than in any of Speare's children's novels. Thus the reader gets to see not only her growth through childhood but also her development as a woman. Through her the reader gets to see the changes in other characters as well over the years, with the emphasis on adult life rather than on youth. In the earlier novels the reader sees the maturation process but not the adult that the process will create; there are implications only about the futures of Miriam, Kit, Daniel, and later Matt. In *The Prospering* the reader primarily sees the emotional conflicts of adults, observing how their weaknesses mix with their strengths as they try to accept what life offers them. The French and Indian War also plays a part in the novel, revealing a side of Eph's character previously unseen by the reader. The war's influence is felt on all of the characters through various incidents involving Indians and the soldiers stationed in the town. Here the focus is quite different from that in *Calico Captive*, which begins a couple of years later, 1754, than the last section before the epilogue in *The Prospering*, "Stockbridge: 1752."

Critical Reception

Although "the book went out of print in no time" (Interview), as adult books frequently do, it received praise from reviewers. The reviewer in *Best Seller* called it "an excellently woven novel. . . . There are some characters starkly and beautifully portrayed" (Marguerite, 102). G. F. Dole noted that "her careful research is evident in her latest book, which moves along at a steady pace. . . . The characters are excellently drawn."[5] In the acknowledgments Speare lists several of the books that were crucial to her research, giving the reader an opportunity to learn more about the founding of Stockbridge and its inhabitants.

There were critical suggestions from the beginning from Anne Barrett after she had read the manuscript. "My interest began to lag after David Brainerd's death. . . . this may be partly because some of the participants remain shadowy—Timothy Woodbridge, for instance. . . . I have no real feeling for him as a person" (Barrett 1). In her next letter to Speare, Barrett reiterated, "I have almost no feeling of Woodbridge as a person and so, no conviction about the motives behind his actions" (Barrett 2). Barrett then raised a series of questions that she thought Speare might wish to address, such as "What does Elizabeth think of him [Woodbridge]? How much is he influenced by the envy of the Williamses? by disgust at Ephraim's sharp practices? by resentment of his wife's whininess and inefficiency? How real is his religious conviction? Does he use it (perhaps unconsciously) as a weapon in a personal feud? Is he a good but limited and bigoted man? A religious zealot? Also, who are the members of his faction?" (Barrett 2). Barrett's last observation on the subject is that "I want to know more about Woodbridge and about some of the other members of the community" (Barrett 2).

Some of these questions are answered after the death of John Sergeant. "The Indians found a voice in Timothy Woodbridge. They had always trusted him, recognizing his simple unshakable honesty. . . . He should not be blamed that somehow his uprightness lacked the persuasion of John Sergeant's. For one thing, he did not have John's indiscriminate trust, and he did not have John's springing optimism. I believe that for many years Timothy had been corroded by suspicion and bitterness. Now the Indians found him all too willing to listen to grievances that John had always managed to smooth over" (*P*, 249). Speare tells how the old families lined up behind Williams while the newer arrivals took Woodbridge's side. When a new minister, Ezra Stiles, comes for a trial period and stays with Abigail, the reader and Liza learn that Woodbridge, according to Abigail, has accused John Sergeant of being an Arminian, "that he preached salvation by good works rather than by election" (*P*, 256). A discussion of Arminianism follows. Stiles mentions his own doubts about New Light doctrine, doubts which somehow get to Woodbridge who is then instrumental in delaying an invitation to Stiles to be the permanent minister at Stockbridge. The Woodbridge-Williams feud grows as Speare gives the reader more glimpses of their opposing positions. Later, after Liza has gone to school in Boston and returns for Abigail's wedding to General Dwight, she discovers more of a split between the two factions. Now the Williamses no longer even go to Sunday meetings (where Jonathan Edwards is minister) because of the bitter divisions.

Future Plans

When asked if she had had thoughts of writing another book for adults since she had enjoyed the work on *The Prospering* so thoroughly, Speare replied: "After I finished *The Prospering*, I decided I wanted to do an adult biography, and I worked four or five years on it, but nobody wanted it. . . . I could see that it was not going to be a big seller, and that's what they needed, especially Houghton Mifflin who is one of the few publishers that stayed out of mergers" (Interview). Still, she persisted. "I tried an agent and she sent it to two or three other places, and then I just abandoned it. It was a biography of Fanny Kemble" (Interview). Although Kemble, an English actress, made quite a sensation in this country and "wrote one of the few first-person witness accounts of slavery in the South" (Interview), after her marriage to an American she discovered that his "income and all of his livelihood was gained from a slave plantation in Georgia" (Interview). Fanny, herself, "was bitterly opposed to slavery. . . . She was a fascinating woman, but there's no sex in the book whatsoever, and she became a rather unlikable person as she grew older" (Interview).

Speare said that she had thought of the possibility of making the Kemble material into a book for older children, but she was skeptical: "Whether older children would want a story of a married woman with children in Georgia (she had two children), I don't know. While the agent had it, one of the big children's book publishers wanted to see it, and I said no, I don't think it's a children's book. I don't think that I could go back and do it now because I've lost track of so much. . . . I would have to read all those diaries of Fanny Kemble's again and find where all my references are. I didn't make any notes" (Interview). Since more than 12 years have passed since her work on the biography, a return to it would require formidable amounts of time and effort.

Speare was asked if she had ever contemplated writing a contemporary novel. "I wouldn't dare try a contemporary novel. I'm sure it would be out of style before I finished it" (Interview). What else might she contemplate writing? "I don't know. I think I've somewhat lost my drive. It takes energy and I don't seem to have that now" (Interview). All that might change, perhaps, if she should happen upon another historical incident that will not let go of her imagination and that will plunge her once more into one of her favorite occupations, research. Readers have that possibility to hope for, but for the present Speare has already given them a legacy of memorable settings, characters, plots, and strong themes for the enjoyment and benefit of many generations to come.

Conclusion

Historical fiction, especially in the past few decades, has been dwindling steadily in popularity. Jean Fritz, renowned writer of historical fiction and biographies for young readers, has commented that "some young people have the tendency to shrug off the study of history as irrelevant. On the other hand, I feel that a society, as well as an individual, has to come to terms with its past before it can either profit from it or be released from it."[1] Other writers and most educated people have felt the same way. Unless we know and understand the past, we are doomed to repeat the mistakes we have made. An interesting way to learn how the average person and family reacted during a particular period in history is through the reading of good historical fiction.

Elizabeth Speare was writing during the beginning of and rise in popularity of the realistic "modern problem" novel, books that not only dealt with divorce and single-parent homes but also eventually tackled such formerly taboo subjects as rape, incest, child abuse, desertion by the mother, AIDS, and many other salable topics. Many of Speare's own early articles were on contemporary, timely subjects, as was her play, *The Anchor*. Yet throughout the period of her major publications, from 1957 to 1983, she stuck fast to her own growing interests in history and to her beliefs, even as children were clamoring for the latest Judy Blume book or one by Norma Klein, M. E. Kerr, the Cleavers, and countless others whose forte was realistic fiction. These writers catered to the child's curiosity about the problems of growing up. During this period the popularity of historical fiction decreased noticeably in libraries and in bookstores. Instead, young readers were flocking to books about modern children and families in contemporary settings with problems they had heard about, witnessed, or experienced firsthand.

Although the often heavily serious realism of the sixties and seventies began to take on more humor in the eighties, the contemporary realistic trend continued. As Hugh Crago has observed, "Television's children are virtually deprived of history; the past, even the comparatively recent past, is not very real to them, and most of them are curiously incurious about it."[2] The present and the immediate future are all that matters. This situation is particularly unfortunate for today's child, who is often caught up in an increasingly rootless society where families move frequently, removing children from close relatives, or where the family itself disintegrates at times, even causing the separation of siblings. As Rosemary Sutcliff, the noted British writer of historical fiction, observes in her article "History Is People": "I feel it to be enormously important that the young should be given this sense of continuity, that they should be given the feeling of their roots behind them. To know and really understand something of where one came from helps one to understand and cope better with where one is now—and where one is going to."[3] In today's mobile society, her points are especially well taken.

On the surface, then, Speare's books would appear to be anachronistic, set in earlier periods that no longer seem to interest children. Yet despite—or, perhaps, because of—the trend away from historical fiction that still persists among young readers, Speare's work takes on added significance in a contemporary world filled with unrest and uncertainty, in which the future of the planet itself is disturbingly unclear. Hugh Crago maintains that "it is vital that there be as many people as possible growing up with a vivid consciousness of where we came from, in order to neither over-dramatize nor to underrate the present crisis of our species and its world" (Crago, 100). Writers of historical fiction should not give in to the popular trends of the moment; they should instead persist in writing about what is most important to them, in the genre in which they are most at ease.

Speare also recognizes that "the world into which our children are about to step is filled with peril," and she cautions adults that "in our anxiety to prepare our children for the Space Age, we must make very sure that they do not miss those imaginary adventures which so greatly illumine and enrich their lives."[4] She also feels strongly that "children need books for the heart as well as for the mind. . . . When a story stirs us deeply, for a moment at least we realize these qualities [of courage, devotion, compassion, forgiveness] in ourselves" (Kingman, 77). Young people must be given values to hold onto and to live by; those values are often submerged in pessimism in realistic fiction, as in S. E. Hinton's *That Was Then, This Is Now* or Robert Cormier's *The Chocolate War.* In contrast, supportive and reassuring moral codes can be found in Speare's books without the sacrifice of a fascinating story. She continues the didactic tradition in its best sense, a feature that has been a part of children's literature since its inception and that persists in many fine books for young readers today.

It is precisely because of the moral values Speare incorporates into her books, together with universal themes and sharply delineated characters, that she has an assured place in children's literature, a very high place. Although historical fiction has a way of going out of fashion periodically, Speare's books have a timeless quality and a durability, especially *The Witch of Blackbird Pond* and *The Sign of the Beaver,* that make them suitable for any generation. She focuses on the indomitable human spirit, on the resilience and courage of the individual under duress, and she offers her readers through her fiction the hope that life will be better. Erik Haugaard, in his two-part essay for *Horn Book,* states that "even though our computer-run society seems superficially so different from any that humanity has constructed before, our dreams and ambitions have not changed."[5] Speare focuses on the universal values that link past, present, and future.

Speare also demonstrates that people do not succeed alone, that they need each other for moral support and, at times, for physical help as well. This is especially important now when children are often left to fend for themselves in fiction and when the plight of the homeless and other problems have become evident to all through media attention. Such remote happenings become real possibilities to some children when parents lose their jobs and begin to fall behind on house payments. Haugaard states that "a knowledge and a feeling for the history of mankind makes you realize that others have lived before you—dreamed, loved, plotted, failed, or won. This gives a perspective to your own life, makes you aware that time passes, that every minute the present becomes the past and becomes history" (Haugaard, 705). The struggles of families today will be the memories of tomorrow.

Speare, through her historical fiction, offers her readers hope, but not without struggle and help, as both Kit in *The Witch of Blackbird Pond* and Matt in *The Sign of the Beaver* demonstrate in their dependence upon others for survival until they reach a point where they can cope on their own. In Kit's case, she goes from the protection of the Wood household to life with Nat Eaton, rather than to completely independent living even for a short time as was the case with Matt. Yet she has shown enough independence of spirit throughout, even in choosing Nat, for the reader to realize that she will not be a meek, yea-saying wife. Miriam Willard in *Calico Captive* and Daniel in *The Bronze Bow* also must depend upon family and friends despite their strong, independent characters; Speare seems to be saying that family members must support and sustain each other, and that independence, though good, cannot entirely replace the need for connection.

In her work Elizabeth Speare reveals the strong religious foundation of her life that has evoked in her a potent need for fairness to others, evidenced in the objectivity toward various groups and religions that she tries to instill in her books. Her characters are essentially moral ones, even some of those who are cast as antagonists. Thus Dr. Bulkeley in *The Witch of Blackbird Pond* comes off well despite Matthew Wood's disagreements with him, especially when he shows his compassionate, caring side in helping Mercy over her illness; and Mehkoa acts the way many young men still do, teasing the object of their affections and then watching to see what the reaction will be.[6] *The Bronze Bow*, of course, reveals Speare's religious attitudes most clearly of all her books for young readers and boldly affirms the power of love, which is a theme in her other novels as well. Her strong love of her own family and their closeness is also carried into the novels, adding to their strength. Her presentations of loving family groups offers hope to the reader, even to those from broken and disadvantaged homes, that love can be found—and if not in present circumstances, then perhaps in future ones.

In writing *The Prospering*, Speare has shown the connection between literature for children and literature for adults. She has demonstrated that although religious philosophy and human natures can be explored in greater depth as the characters mature in her adult novel, essentially the same process is carried out in each: the thorough research, the crafting of characters both from real life and from her imagination, and the re-creation of plot from the research into captivating tales that focus on the individual's reaction to the difficulties life presents. In both novels for young readers and novels for adults, her strong moral values shine through, sustaining the characters. The differences between *The Prospering* and the other novels lie in the degree of introspection and the amount of religious discussion the works contain rather than with additions or subtractions purposely made for adults or for children. She regards her dual audiences almost as equals, except for certain interests and experiences, rather than as two completely separate groups. This is a remarkable attitude shared only by the best writers.

Through her novels in particular, but not exclusively, Elizabeth George Speare has shown that history in fiction can be exciting and fascinating and can bring a period to life in ways no textbooks can match. In his chapter "The Nature of History," Herbert J. Muller stated that "our age is notorious for its want of piety or sense of the past; up-to-date men have been too busy making gadgets, automobiles, depressions, and wars to care much about anything older than the minutes of the last meeting" (Muller, 27). Through her fiction Speare shows that the past contained people very like those of the present, who also faced similar dilemmas and tried to respond with strength and courage. Using her imagination, coupled with a talent for creating memorable, morally courageous characters, Elizabeth George Speare has given readers lasting works of literature that stimulate thought and contain characters with which young readers may identify for generations to come.

In her writing, Speare eschews melodrama to concentrate on the choices her strong individuals must make under difficult circumstances. In view of this emphasis on strength of character in her novels, Speare was a fitting selection for the first winner of the Scott O'Dell Historical Fiction Award in 1984, given for her last book to date, *The Sign of the Beaver*. She has demonstrated that historical fiction is not about something that happened "way back then" but is especially relevant to readers today who have many more options and thus more decisions to make in their own lives. Erik Haugaard writes that "just as the past casts its shadow into the future, so does the present bear upon the historian's study of the past. History is what we choose to recall" (Haugaard, 700). Speare has chosen to present history through the individual rather than through major events; the hiding of the Connecticut Charter is the closest she comes to a great historical event in her novels. Even the French and Indian War serves only as a background catalyst for the events in *Calico Captive*, though later it makes a slightly stronger impression in *The Prospering*. This overall focus on character gives the reader a more intimate feeling for the people who lived generations ago and paves the way for self-discovery in the process. Elizabeth George Speare's historical fiction has the ability to give modern readers a better understanding of their own lives. Beyond that, in each book she wanted to tell an absorbing story, and time after time she has succeeded admirably.

Notes and References

Chapter One

1. Mary Silva Cosgrave, "Elizabeth George Speare," *Horn Book* 65, no. 4 (July–August 1989): 466.

2. Elizabeth George Speare, *Elizabeth George Speare* (Boston: Houghton Mifflin, n.d.), n.p.; hereafter cited in text as Booklet.

3. Elizabeth George Speare, "Autobiographical Sketch," in *More Junior Authors,* ed. Muriel Fuller (New York: H. W. Wilson, 1963), 189; hereafter cited in text as *MJA.*

4. Elizabeth George Speare, telephone conversation with author, 27 April 1990; hereafter cited in text as Telephone conversation.

5. Elizabeth George Speare, letter to author, 23 April 1990; hereafter cited in text as Letter 2.

6. Elizabeth George Speare, letter to author, 12 April 1990; hereafter cited in text as Letter 1.

7. Speare donated typescripts and other materials to the Mugar Memorial Library at Boston University where they are kept in Special Collections. Along with galleys of *Calico Captive, The Witch of Blackbird Pond, The Bronze Bow, Life in Colonial America,* and *The Ice Glen (The Prospering)* is an early typescript of *The Ice Glen* from two points of view, plus a second draft of *The Bronze Bow* with a different beginning from the final version. The typescripts are usually on scrap paper or old, yellowed paper. A study of the corrections reveals that Speare was always polishing her prose.

8. Helen Reeder Cross, "Biographical Note: Elizabeth George Speare," in *Newbery and Caldecott Medal Books: 1956–1965,* ed. Lee Kingman (Boston: Horn Book, 1965), 79; hereafter cited in text.

9. Elizabeth George Speare, interview with author at Speare's home in Easton, Conn., 12 July 1989; hereafter cited in text as Interview.

10. Elizabeth George Speare, "Author's Commentary," in *Children's Literature Review,* ed. Gerard J. Senick (Detroit: Gale Research, 1985), 205; hereafter cited in text as *CLR.*

11. Jean Fritz, "The Very Truth," in *Celebrating Children's Books: Essays on Children's Literature in Honor of Zena Sutherland,* ed. Betsy

Hearne and Marilyn Kaye (New York: Lothrop, Lee & Shepard, 1981), 83; hereafter cited in text.

12. Both books were published the year the Speares moved to Easton, Conn., where they still live.

13. Milton Meltzer, "Beyond the Span of a Single Life," in *Celebrating Children's Books: Essays on Children's Literature in Honor of Zena Sutherland,* ed. Betsy Hearne and Marilyn Kaye (New York: Lothrop, Lee & Shepard, 1981), 88; hereafter cited in text.

Chapter Two

1. Elizabeth George, "Don't Be an Armchair Eskimo," *Better Homes and Gardens* 28, no. 4 (December 1949): 150–52; hereafter cited in text as *BHG.*

2. Elizabeth George Speare, "Outwitting the Therbligs," *Woman's Day* (April 1963): 35, 175–76; hereafter cited in text as *WD.*

3. Elizabeth G. Speare, "Abby, Julia, and the Cows," *American Heritage* 8, no. 4 (June 1957): 54–57, 96; hereafter cited in text as *AH.*

4. Elizabeth George Speare, "Old-Time Schoolmasters and Scholars," *The New England Galaxy* 1, no. 4 (Spring 1960); 6–15; hereafter cited in text as *Galaxy.*

5. Elizabeth George Speare, *The Anchor: A Play in One Act for Four Women* (Boston: Baker's, 1953); hereafter cited in text as *Anchor.*

6. Elizabeth George Speare, letter to author, 15 May 1990; hereafter cited in text as Letter 3.

7. Elizabeth George Speare, *The Stranger: A One Act Play of Bible Times* (Boston: W. H. Baker, 1955); hereafter cited in text as *Stranger.*

8. The description of the costumes worn by the characters follows the final curtain. The dress of men and women are the same except for color; only Jacob wears a shortened tunic because of his age.

Chapter Three

1. Walter Hard, "Mrs. Johnson Remembers," in *The Connecticut,* illus. Douglas W. Gorsline (New York: Rinehart, 1947), 119–34; hereafter cited in text.

2. A reviewer mistakenly places the opening scenes in Vermont. See "Calico Captive," *Virginia Kirkus' Service* 25, no. 18 (15 September 1957); 693.

3. Susanna Willard Johnson Hastings, *A Narrative of the Captivity of Mrs. Johnson* (Walpole, N.H.: David Carlisle, Jr., 1796); reprinted as vol. 23 of *The Garland Library of Narratives of North American Indian Captivities*, selected and arranged by Wilcomb E. Washburn (New York: Garland, 1976), 1–144; hereafter cited in text as Hastings. Farnsworth, a hired man also captured in the diary, is omitted from *Calico Captive*.

4. "Elizabeth George Speare," in *Something about the Author*, ed. Anne Commire, vol. 5 (Detroit: Gale Research, 1973), 178; hereafter cited in text as *SAA*.

5. Elizabeth George Speare, "Laura Ingalls Wilder Award Acceptance," *Horn Book* 65, no. 4 (July–August 1989), 461; hereafter cited in text as *HB* 1989.

6. Mary Silva Cosgrave, letter to Elizabeth George Speare, 2 October 1956; hereafter cited in text as Cosgrave 1.

7. Eudora Welty, *Place in Fiction* (New York: House of Books, 1957), n.p.; hereafter cited in text. The book is "a condensation of lectures prepared for the Conference on American Studies in Cambridge, England, in 1954."

8. Margaret Sherwood Libby, review of *Calico Captive*, by Elizabeth George Speare, *New York Herald Tribune*, 17 November 1957, Book Review section.

9. D. C. Muecke, *Irony and the Ironic* (London: Methuen, 1970; reprint, New York: Methuen, 1982); all citations refer to the 1982 edition.

10. Rosemary Sprague, "Biography: The Other Side of the Coin," in *Horn Book Reflections: On Children's Books and Reading*, ed. Elinor Whitney Field (Boston: Horn Book, 1969), 128.

11. Elizabeth George Speare, *Calico Captive* (Boston: Houghton Mifflin, 1957), 258; hereafter cited in text as *CC*.

12. Frank G. Speck, *Penobscot Man: The Life History of a Forest Tribe in Maine* (Philadelphia: University of Pennsylvania Press, 1940); hereafter cited in the text.

13. Conrad Richter, *The Light in the Forest* (New York: Knopf, 1953).

14. According to Hard, "Two tablets beside the road, between Weathersfield [sic] and Reading, Vermont, recall the birth of this baby although the spot where the booth [the shelter constructed by the Indians for the birth] stood is some distance away in the town of Cavendish" (Hard, 128).

15. Vivian J. Scheinmann, "Elizabeth George Speare," in *Twentieth Century Children's Writers*, ed. D. L. Kirkpatrick (New York: St. Martin's Press, 1978), 1156; hereafter cited in text.

16. Review of *Calico Captive*, by Elizabeth George Speare, *Bulletin of the Children's Book Center* 11, no. 4 (December 1957): 48.

17. Review of *Calico Captive,* by Elizabeth George Speare, *Junior Bookshelf* 27, no. 5 (November 1963): 304.

18. Hester Burton, "The Writing of Historical Novels," in *Children and Literature: Views and Reviews,* ed. Virginia Haviland (Glenview, Ill.: Scott, Foresman, 1973), 303; hereafter cited in text.

Chapter Four

1. Interview. Those wishing to see a little of Wethersfield and the interior of the Williams house can order the videotape cassette, "A Visit with Elizabeth George Speare" (Boston: Houghton Mifflin, n.d.), Author and Artist Series 5-96426, VHS.

2. Mary Silva Cosgrave, letter to Elizabeth George Speare, 4 September 1957; hereafter cited in text as Cosgrave 2.

3. Mary Silva Cosgrave, letter to Elizabeth George Speare, 24 March 1958; hereafter cited in text as Cosgrave 3.

4. Another book, *Tituba of Salem Village* by Ann Petry (New York: Crowell, 1964), also has its protagonist come from Barbados to Puritan New England. See Donna E. Morton, *Through the Eyes of a Child: An Introduction to Children's Literature* (Columbus, Ohio: Merrill, 1987), 483–85, for discussion and comparison of the Petry and Speare novels.

5. Elizabeth George Speare, *The Witch of Blackbird Pond* (Boston: Houghton Mifflin, 1958), 25; hereafter cited in text as *WBP.*

6. Samuel Lucas, *Charters of the Old English Colonies in America* (London: John W. Parker, 1850), 47; hereafter cited in text.

7. According to Wright, Massachusetts gave up its charter in 1684. See Louis B. Wright, *The Cultural Life of the American Colonies, 1607–1763* (New York: Harper & Row, 1957), 83; hereafter cited in text.

8. Feminists on Children's Literature, "A Feminist Look at Children's Books," *School Library Journal,* an appendix to *Library Journal* 17, no. 5 (January 1971): 22.

9. Judith Adell and Hilary Dole Klein, comps., *A Guide to Non-sexist Children's Books* (Chicago: Academy Chicago, 1976), 107.

10. Barbara H. Baskin and Karen H. Harris, *Notes from a Different Drummer: A Guide to Juvenile Fiction Portraying the Handicapped* (New York: R. R. Bowker, 1977), 305. The entry is included in the chapter, "An Annotated Guide to Juvenile Fiction Portraying the Handicapped, 1940–1975," 304–305; hereafter cited in text as Baskin and Harris.

11. M[argaret] S[herwood] Libby, review of *The Witch of Blackbird Pond,* by Elizabeth George Speare, *New York Herald Tribune,* 2 November 1958), Book Review Section, 20.

Chapter Five

1. Elizabeth George Speare, *The Bronze Bow* (Boston: Houghton Mifflin, 1961); hereafter cited in the text as *BB*.

2. It is interesting that no one has criticized Speare's presentation of a black man acting as a devoted slave to Daniel and giving up his life for the young man. Such criticism was leveled at Theodore Taylor's *The Cay* (Garden City, N.Y.: Doubleday, 1969) in which a black man, Timothy, gives up his life for the young boy, Phillip, after teaching the boy to be independent despite his blindness.

3. Margaret Sherwood Libby, review of *The Bronze Bow*, by Elizabeth George Speare, *New York Herald Tribune*, 12 November 1961, Books section.

4. Herbert J. Muller, *The Uses of the Past* (New York: Oxford University Press, 1952), 40; hereafter cited in text.

5. Jason Epstein, "'Good Bunnies Always Obey': Books for American Children," in *Only Connect: Readings on Children's Literature*, ed. Sheila Egoff, G. T. Stubbs, and L. F. Ashley (New York: Oxford University Press, 1980), 80; hereafter cited in text.

Chapter Six

1. Marion Jacques Smith, *A History of Maine: From Wilderness to Statehood* (Portland, Me: Falmouth Publishing House, 1949), 263–64; hereafter cited in text. I am indebted to Elizabeth George Speare for having sent me a copy of Smith's account of the incident.

2. Elizabeth George Speare, "The Survival Story," *Horn Book* 64, no. 2 (March–April 1988): 163–64; hereafter cited in text as "Survival."

3. Elizabeth George Speare, *The Sign of the Beaver* (Boston: Houghton Mifflin, 1983), 27; hereafter cited in text as *SB*.

4. Walter Lorraine, Director, Children's Trade Books at Houghton Mifflin, letter to Elizabeth George Speare, 2 February 1982; hereafter cited in text as Lorraine.

5. Review of *The Sign of the Beaver*, by Elizabeth George Speare, *Junior Bookshelf* 43, no. 3 (June 1984): 145.

6. Jean Fritz, review of *The Sign of the Beaver*, by Elizabeth George Speare, *New York Times*, 8 May 1983, Book Review section.

7. Barbara Elleman, review of *The Sign of the Beaver*, by Elizabeth George Speare, *Booklist* 79, no. 16 (15 April 1983): 1098.

Chapter Seven

1. Elizabeth George Speare, *Child Life in New England, 1790–1840* (Sturbridge, Mass.: Old Sturbridge Village, 1961), 3; hereafter cited in text as *CLNE*. Since the booklet is no longer in print, readers might wish to see Jack Larkin, *Children Everywhere: Dimensions of Childhood in Early Nineteenth-Century New England* (Sturbridge, Mass.: Old Sturbridge Village, 1987), or visit the village, "an outdoor living history museum. Its collections, exhibits, and programs present the story of everyday life in a small New England town during the years from 1790 to 1840" (Museum Fact Sheet 1990).

2. Alice Morse Earle, *Child Life in Colonial Days* (New York: Macmillan, 1899; reprint, Detroit: Gale Research, 1982), 24; hereafter cited in text.

3. Edward Everett Hale, *A New England Boyhood* (New York: Cassell Publishing Company, 1893), 53–54; hereafter cited in text.

4. Lucy Larcom, *A New England Girlhood* (Boston: Houghton Mifflin, 1882); hereafter cited in text.

Chapter Eight

1. Margaret Sherwood Libby, review of *Life in Colonial America,* by Elizabeth George Speare, *Book Week,* 10 November 1963, 20.

2. Alice Dalgliesh, review of *Life in Colonial America,* by Elizabeth George Speare, *Saturday Review* 46 (14 December 1963): 50; hereafter cited in text.

3. Elizabeth George Speare, *Life in Colonial America,* illus. Charles Walker (New York: Random House, 1963), Publisher's Note; hereafter cited in text as *LCA*.

4. Paul Fleischman, *Saturnalia* (New York: Harper & Row, 1990), 4. Fleischman also states that "like the town's other tithingmen, he had spiritual charge of ten families, noting with care their attendance at services and testing their children's knowledge of Scripture" (5).

5. Edward Tunis, *Colonial Living* (New York: World, 1957); hereafter cited in text.

6. M[argaret] S[herwood] Libby, "Our Past in Present Tense," *Sunday Herald Tribune,* 10 November 1963, Book Review section.

7. Review of *Life in Colonial America,* by Elizabeth George Speare, *Kirkus* 31, no. 20 (15 October 1963): 1009.

8. Review of *Life in Colonial America,* by Elizabeth George Speare, *Christian Science Monitor,* 14 November 1963.

9. Esther Swift, review of *Life in Colonial America,* by Elizabeth

George Speare, *Library Journal* 88, no. 20 (15 November 1963): 4489; hereafter cited in text.

10. Zena Sutherland, review of *Life in Colonial America,* by Elizabeth George Speare, *Bulletin of the Center for Children's Books* 17, no. 4 (December 1963): 65.

Chapter Nine

1. Elizabeth George Speare, *The Prospering* (Boston: Houghton Mifflin, 1967), vi; hereafter cited in text as *P.*
2. Anne N. Barrett, Editor, Houghton Mifflin, letter to Elizabeth George Speare, 25 January 1966; hereafter cited in text as Barrett 1.
3. Sister M. Marguerite, review of *The Prospering,* by Elizabeth George Speare, *Best Seller* 27 (1 June 1967): 102; hereafter cited in text.
4. Anne N. Barrett, letter to Elizabeth George Speare, 2 February 1966; hereafter cited in text as Barrett 2.
5. G. F. Dole, review of *The Prospering,* by Elizabeth George Speare, *Library Journal* 92 (1 June 1967): 2665.

Conclusion

1. Jean Fritz, "Make Room for the Eighteenth Century," *Horn Book* 50, no. 5 (October 1974): 180.
2. Hugh Crago, "Creation to Civilization," *Signal* 41 (May 1983): 100; hereafter cited in text.
3. Rosemary Sutcliff, "History Is People," in *Children and Literature,* ed. Virginia Haviland (Glenview, Ill.: Scott, Foresman, 1973), 311.
4. Elizabeth George Speare, "Newbery Medal Acceptance," in *Newbery and Caldecott Medal Books: 1956–1965,* ed. Kingman, 76–77; hereafter cited in text as Kingman.
5. Erik Christian Haugaard, "'Before I Was Born': History and the Child," part 2, *Horn Book* 55, no. 6 (December 1979): 705; hereafter cited in text.
6. When I was in sixth grade, a male classmate and a group of his friends chased me home from school one day. My mother called his mother, then spoke to him and asked him why he did such a thing; he replied, "Because I like her." Some things never change.

Selected Bibliography

Primary Works

Novels

The Bronze Bow. Boston: Houghton Mifflin, 1961.
Calico Captive. Illus. W. T. Mars. Boston: Houghton Mifflin, 1957.
The Prospering. Boston: Houghton Mifflin, 1967.
The Sign of the Beaver. Boston: Houghton Mifflin, 1983.
The Witch of Blackbird Pond. Boston: Houghton Mifflin, 1958.

Nonfiction

Child Life in New England, 1790–1840. Sturbridge, Mass.: Old Sturbridge Village, 1961.
Life in Colonial America. Illus. Charles Walker. New York: Random House, 1963.

Plays

"The Forest of Arden." *Plays.* Boston: Plays, Inc., 1952.
The Anchor: A Play in One Act for Four Women. Boston: Baker's, 1953.
The Stranger: A One Act Play of Bible Times. Boston: Baker's, 1955.

Articles

"Abby, Julia, and the Cows." *American Heritage* 8, no. 4 (June 1957): 54–57, 96.
"Don't Be an Armchair Eskimo." *Better Homes and Gardens* 28, no. 4 (December 1949): 150–52.
"Old-Time Schoolmasters and Scholars." *New England Galaxy* 1, no. 4 (Spring 1960): 6–15.
"Outwitting the Therbligs." *Woman's Day* (April 1953): 35, 175–76.

Miscellaneous

A Visit with Elizabeth George Speare. Boston: Houghton Mifflin, Author and Artist Series 5-96426, VHS. This videotaped interview is set in Wethersfield and shows the interior of the restored colonial house used for background information for *The Witch of Blackbird Pond* as well as the meadow at Blackbird Pond. Speare talks about her life and writing.

Secondary Works

Letters

Letters from Mary Silva Cosgrave and Anne N. Barrett are housed in the Elizabeth George Speare Collection, Boston University Libraries.

Books

Adell, Judith, and Klein, Hilary Dole, comps. *A Guide to Non-sexist Children's Books.* Chicago: Academy Chicago, 1976. An annotated bibliography arranged by grades followed by a section for all ages, with a one-page introduction by Alan Alda.

Baskin, Barbara H., and Harris, Karen H. *Notes from a Different Drummer: A Guide to Juvenile Fiction Portraying the Handicapped.* New York: R. R. Bowker, 1977. Four essays on "Society and the Handicapped" and on the handicapped in literature are followed by "An Annotated Guide to Juvenile Fiction Portraying the Handicapped, 1940–1975."

Commire, Ann, ed. "Elizabeth George Speare." In *Something about the Author,* vol. 5. Detroit: Gale Research, 1973. Gives important dates and contains Speare's account of her background, research, and writing habits.

Cross, Helen Reeder. "Biographical Note: Elizabeth George Speare." In *Newbery and Caldecott Medal Books: 1956–1965,* 78–81. Boston: Horn Book, 1965. Talks about the "Quill Drivers" and the group's influence on Speare in addition to other personal information.

Epstein, Jason. "'Good Bunnies Always Obey': Books for American Children." In *Only Connect: Readings on Children's Literature,* 2d ed., edited by Sheila Egoff, G. T. Stubbs, and L. F. Ashley. New York: Oxford University Press, 1980. Makes some general historical comments, attacks pedagogical nature of books, decries recent Newbery Award–winners, laments the mass-market approach to books. In general, disparages the American children's book scene.

Morton, Donna E. "Involving Children in Historical Fiction." In *Through the Eyes of a Child: An Introduction to Children's Literature,* 2d ed. Columbus, Ohio: Merrill, 1987. Morton compares *The Witch of Blackbird Pond* and *Tituba of Salem Village* with suggestions for dramatizing each.

Scheinmann, Vivian. "Elizabeth George Speare." In *Twentieth Century Children's Writers,* edited by D. L. Kirkpatrick. New York: St. Martin's, 1978. Critical commentary on Speare's work.

Speare, Elizabeth George. "Autobiographical Sketch." In *More Junior Authors,* edited by Muriel Fuller. New York: H. W. Wilson, 1963. Gives background information about her life and writing.

Journal Articles

Cosgrave, Mary Silva. "Elizabeth George Speare." *Horn Book* 65 (July–August 1989): 465–68. Talks about her contacts with Speare as Speare's editor and her appreciation of the fine writing.

Feminists on Children's Literature. "A Feminist Look at Children's Books." *School Library Journal,* appendix to *Library Journal* 17, no. 5 (January 1971): 19–24. Describes various ways that books are unacceptable (attitude, cop-out, focus, etc.) from a feminist's point of view.

Speare, Elizabeth George. "Author's Commentary." *Children's Literature Review* 8 (1985): 204–11. Contains an author's commentary before some of the books followed by reviews. Gives personal background and particulars about the writing of the books.

Speare, Elizabeth George. "Laura Ingalls Wilder Award Acceptance." *Horn Book* 65 (July–August 1989): 460–64. Speare tells about her early rejections and Mary Cosgrave's encouragement, then explains her interest in Indians and why she writes historical fiction.

Speare, Elizabeth George. "The Survival Story." *Horn Book* 64 (March–April 1988): 163–72. Gives background for the creation and writing of *The Sign of the Beaver.*

Book Reviews

Calico Captive

Review of *Calico Captive*, by Elizabeth George Speare. *Virginia Kirkus Service* 25, no. 18 (15 September 1957): 693.

Libby, Margaret Sherwood. Review of *Calico Captive*, by Elizabeth George Speare. *New York Herald Tribune*, 17 November 1957, Book Review section.

Review of *Calico Captive*, by Elizabeth George Speare. *Bulletin of the Children's Book Center* 11, no. 4 (December 1957): 48.

Review of *Calico Captive*, by Elizabeth George Speare. *Junior Bookshelf* 27, no. 5 (November 1963): 304.

The Witch of Blackbird Pond

Libby, Margaret Sherwood. Review of *The Witch of Blackbird Pond*, by Elizabeth George Speare. *New York Herald Tribune*, 2 November 1958.

The Bronze Bow

Libby, Margaret Sherwood. Review of *The Bronze Bow*, by Elizabeth George Speare. *New York Herald Tribune*, 12 November 1961.

Viguers, Ruth Hill. Review of *The Bronze Bow*, by Elizabeth George Speare. *Horn Book* 37 (October 1961): 432.

Life in Colonial America

Libby, Margaret Sherwood. Review of *Life in Colonial America*, by Elizabeth George Speare. *Book Week*, 10 November 1963, 20.

Libby, Margaret Sherwood. "Our Past in Present Tense." *Sunday Herald Tribune*, 10 November 1963.

Review of *Life in Colonial America*, by Elizabeth George Speare. *Christian Science Monitor*, 14 November 1963.

Review of *Life in Colonial America*, by Elizabeth George Speare. *Virginia Kirkus' Service* 31, no. 20 (15 October 1963): 1009.

Dalgliesh, Alice. Review of *Life in Colonial America*, by Elizabeth George Speare. *Saturday Review* 46 (14 December 1963): 50.

Sutherland, Zena. Review of *Life in Colonial America*, by Elizabeth George Speare. *Bulletin for the Center of Children's Books* 17, no. 4 (December 1963): 65.

Swift, Esther. Review of *Life in Colonial America*, by Elizabeth George Speare. *Library Journal* 88, no. 20 (15 November 1963): 4489.

The Prospering

Marguerite, Sister M. Review of *The Prospering*, by Elizabeth George Speare. *Best Seller* 27 (1 June 1967): 102.

The Sign of the Beaver

Elleman, Barbara. Review of *The Sign of the Beaver*, by Elizabeth George Speare. *Booklist* 79, no. 16 (15 April 1983): 1098.

Fritz, Jean. Review of *The Sign of the Beaver*, by Elizabeth George Speare. *New York Times*, 8 May 1983.

Review of *The Sign of the Beaver*, by Elizabeth George Speare. *Junior Bookshelf* 43, no. 3 (June 1984): 145.

Index

The Author

Marilyn Apseloff is associate professor of English at Kent State University and specializes in the teaching of children's literature. She attended Bryn Mawr College and the University of Cincinnati, from which she received her B.A. and M.A. She is coauthor, with Celia Catlett Anderson, of *Nonsense Literature for Children: Aesop to Seuss* (1989) and author of *They Wrote for Children Too: An Annotated Bibliography of Children's Books by Famous Writers for Adults* (1989) and a monograph on Virginia Hamilton. She has served as president of the Children's Literature Association, writes the annual "Literature for Children" article for *The World Book Year Book,* and has contributed numerous essays on children's writers for *The World Book Encyclopedia.*

The Editor

Ruth K. MacDonald is a professor of English and head of the Department of English and Philosophy at Purdue University. She received her B.A. and M.A. in English from the University of Connecticut, her Ph.D. in English from Rutgers University, and her M.B.A. from the University of Texas at El Paso. To Twayne's United States and English Authors series she has contributed the volumes on Louisa May Alcott, Beatrix Potter, and Dr. Seuss. She is the author of *Literature for Children in England and America, 1646–1774* (1982).